The 100 Weapons for a Leader

Pius B. Ngeze

TANZANIA EDUCATIONAL PUBLISHERS LTD

Tanzania Educational Publishers Ltd,
TEPU House,
Uganda Road, Plot No. 45 Block MDA,
Mob: +255 685 997583/ +255 758 147871
Email: tepultd@yahoo.com
Website: www.tepu.co.tz
P.O. Box 1222,
Bukoba, Tanzania.

ISBN 978 9987 07 082 4

Table of Contents

PREAMBLE

To be Leader is to be at War all the Time

"In the year 1983, when I was the Kagera Regional CCM Chairman, I compared politics to a football match between two famous and rival football clubs, namely, Yanga and Simba. Today, I would like to inform you that when you become an appointed, selected or elected leader, all the time you are at war. People who are fighting you are some of those whom you don't lead, or/ and some of those under your leadership, who fight (you) to remove you from leadership. They do so by dirtying you, by making a mould of a small issue to be a mountain so that people can see it. You are at war with some of your fellow leaders whom you eat and drink together, because of their own reasons, so that one of them may occupy your position in the next election or in the next period or even before your period of leadership expires, by your leadership being terminated. You are at war with some of the government executives or even fellow politicians who are unhappy with your speed of delivering services and because your leadership performance is threatening their interests. You are at war with some of those who voted you to office and those who did not vote for you by accusing you that you are not performing to their expectations in your leadership. To them, even if you are performing well, they will never see any good thing in you. You are also at war with some people, who even if you are delivering superbly, they will never acknowledge so, always they see no good in you due to the way they see issues and analyse them.

You are attacked by your fellow politicians because of their own interest etc. And these days, you are attacked by politicians from the opposition parties because you are the hindrance to their winning the next elections. For sure, that is the life of a leader, you are always at war.

A politician or any other leader is not supposed to run away from this kind of life or even to lose hope. The one who runs away from this type of life is a coward. Your resolve always should be to live and win the wars. All the time your eyes and ears should be at work. The aim is to win and be victorious.

To me, for a period of 33 years (1974-2007), as a politician, I have lived that kind of life, of being attacked from all directions: South, North, East and West. Today, I am happy to say that I won the wars. However, they are not yet over because I am still alive. I wish each and every one of you to live such kind of life, but you should win them."

Pius B. Ngeze

From My Farewell Speech as the Regional CCM Chairman, Kagera region, on 10/09/2007.

INTRODUCTION

The Meaning of a Leader

A leader is any person, a man or woman, with power or authority over one or more people. Another meaning of a leader is a person who was given an authority to lead a single person or many people. That single person may be a fellow matrimonial partner or a fellow person whom you co-operate with. "Many people" may start from his/her family members up to the whole nation. In other words, **leadership** is the authority of leading one or more than one person for a specific reason. That reason may be developmental, matrimonial, political or liberational in nature, to that person or people.

Leadership in any society is of great importance and of necessity. Once there is an association or existence of at least two people, there must be a leader to lead the other person or others, otherwise, there will be no peace at all or no development of any kind. Even for some kinds of animals, there is a system of having leaders for their groups. In this book, the word "leader" includes:

- Family and clan leaders.

- Political leaders from grassroots to the top.

- Government leaders: President, Members of Parliament, Councilors etc.

- Religion leaders: Pope, Bishops, Priests ,Pastors, Sheikhs, Imams, etc

- Leaders of work: Heads of sections, Heads of departments, Head of Ministry, Managers, Directors, Deputy Directors etc.

- Co-operative leaders: Head of co-operatives unions, co-operative societies, AMCOS, SACCOS, SACCA etc.

- Leaders of government Agencies.

- Traditional leaders.

- Leaders of Nongovernmental organizations.

- Leaders of any kind that I didn't mention.

A person may get leadership by being elected into office by votes. Such leaders are those with government or/ and positions or rank, example; President, Members of Parliament, village chairmen and chairmen of sub-villages, Council chairpersons, District chairperson, Regional chairpersons and delegates of meetings that are led by these leaders.

Other leaders who are voted for are those of religious groups of Protestants and Moslems leaders as well as those of Non- governmental organizations.

There are leaders who are not voted into office for they are appointed by a person or authority that was given the power to do so that by laws, regulations as well as procedures or formalities that are in place. Nevertheless, that appointment is made after consultations, getting the advice from responsible people. Some of the leaders who are appointed are those in government, Cardinals, Bishops, Parish Priests and Pastors, who are given areas or institutions to lead.

However, there is a kind of leadership which you get by being given a position, for example, when a man marries, automatically becomes a leader of the family. When a person is ordained a priest or pastor, automatically he is a spiritual father or leader of his or her followers in his locality etc.

These groups are some of the types of leaders who are the subject of this book. There are some other groups of leaders which I didn't mention, however, they will benefit from this book.

The former President of Tanzania, His Excellence Ali Hassan Mwinyi, when he was president, is quoted to have said, "The untainted man is the one that has not yet married." It is true, when you contest to be elected a leader for the first time, you enter leadership being the cleanest person, without a dirty. Those who elected you, did so having faith in you, believing you will continue being the same clean person you have been: a good leader, a clean leader, without a dirty and scandal, unless if you got that leadership through corrupt means. The same applies to a couple in courtships. A fiancée sees and believes that her fiancé is of the best quality, good-hearted, trustful, humble and good tempered, whom she has no single doubt on any of the qualities. Now, wait till when you become his wife and especially after the oath in the church that no divorce till death!

So, you begin leadership with the high expectations from the people you are leading. To political leaders, your voters or the appointing authority hope that:

- You will lead people to work hard for their own development.

- You will be close to them in joy and hardships.

- You will be their role model in behavior, conduct, character, hardworking etc.

- You will speak on their behalf and defend them.

The main question is whether you will continue to be their mirror or role model for the whole period of your leadership.

However, reality is not that way. After being elected or appointed as a leader, you immediately start to taint yourself or being tainted by other people. You begin a journey of attacks and you defend yourself from these attacks from your enemies. In short, when you get leadership, you have immediately entered the battleground. Wars start on you. War is war, you may win them or lose it. Should you win, your friends and those who support you will rejoice. When you lose the war, your enemies will rejoice and your supporters will be disappointed.

The Meaning of Weapons

On the other hand, Weapons as used in this book, are ethics that defend or protect your personal safety, safety of your leadership, or hinderance to those people who do not wish you well and who will do everything in their means to see to it that you fall off from you current leadership. So, it is logical that you have weapons so that you can win the wars against you or defend yourself from the attacks.

The **Weapons** that are discussed in this book are not objects such as dagger, sword, gun, bomb etc. They are ethics that build a leader, his actions, behaviuor, character and temperament. These weapons are bigger, heavier and more effective than a gun, pistol, baton, arrows, bombs and more others.

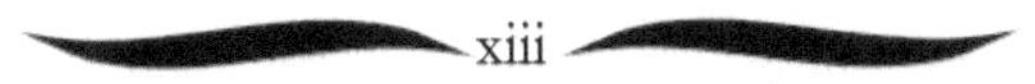

This book is the result of research and my own experience in family leadership for over 35 years, 38 years of leadership at work and 33 years of political leadership. I even contested for elected leadership: won 6 times and lost 2 times. For this reason, I know the joy and comfort of winning a contested election. Also, I know the grief and pain of losing an election.

During the time of my leadership, there are many mistakes that I made and there are many good things that I achieved. During these periods of leadership, I have also learnt of or witnessed mistakes made by other leaders, including political leaders falling and others continuing to lead, but, some being covered with dirty, shame etc. These leaders include religious leaders of the main sects, government leaders, institutional leaders, company leaders, leaders of non-government organizations and leaders of government agencies. The leaders also include those of families and clans.

You, as a leader, if you read, understand and implement these weapons, your enemies will have no reason to begin attacking you. However, attacks on you will not disappear all together, but will be weak and less harmful to your leadership.

I advise people who are not leaders also to read this book so that they understand the weapons made for their leaders.

This is a book which every leader must have. This book, in itself is a Weapon. Weapons should not stay far from you.

It's my hope that this book will be of great importance to leaders of different kinds, together with citizens whom they lead. If at all this book brings some change in perceptions, behaviour, thoughts and character of a leader or leaders and leaders-to-be, it will be have contributed to the positive development and morals of citizens and leaders of countries.

I dedicate this book to all people who will read it and adhere to its contents.

11, May, 2008   *Pius B. Ngeze*

Bukoba, Tanzania.

Weapon 1

Know Yourself

Knowing yourself is to discover and know who you are regarding to your abilities to lead, your good, strong and weak qualities, your weaknesses and strengths etc. Every person has talents given to him by God and knowledge acquired through education and training. Use them to make success of the type of leadership that you have or which you will entrust with.

Know very well your weaknesses and strengths. Which special talents have you got? Use such qualities, good and bad to know yourself. After knowing yourself, confess your weaknesses to your family members or close friends and use your intelligence, bodily abilities, behaviour, character and temperament to make a success of your leadership.

In this world, there is no leader who is perfect, without any weakness. However, a good leader is the one who confesses his weaknesses and promises to get rid of them or to work on them.

A good leader is the one who applies for a certain leadership after he/she has carefully considered his abilities and qualifications to see if he is able and fit for the type of leadership he is contesting. Not everyone can be a president of nation. Not every person can be a member of parliament. Not everyone can be a chairman of political party, a professor etc.

It is not wise to apply for certain type of leadership, which when you mention it, you even surprise your family members. The criteria to put into consideration when choosing the type of leadership to contest, include the level of education having in mind the area or location you live in, your experience, your level of acceptance by people, your family and clan history in your locality, your good and bad weaknesses, your abilities, your strength and your stand on important issues, concerning your people you intend to lead.

To be a leader is not an easy task. It is huge work, heavy responsibility. There are people who fail to lead others, but others manage.

Weapon 2

You should Know very well the Area and the People you Lead

Every leader leads people in a certain geographical area. That area may be a home of a family, hamlet, ward, street, division, county, constituency, district or nation. It may also be a company, diocese, church, state, mosque, parish, political party, co-operative union, a society or an NGO.

You are supposed to read, learn and inquire details about it, so that you get to know well your area of leadership. Understand its history, geography, its boundaries as well as its divisions. Know the leaders who lead the area before you, their achievements and failures.

Also, know the people of that area, whom you will lead: their history, their culture, their level of educational status, their agriculture, culture, customs, traditions etc.

Once you know well the area you are leading and its people or people who work in that area; it becomes easy for you to lead them, to speak on their behalf and to plead for them. But, you should not stop to understand them, because behaviuors of people change, depending on the period of time and certain events. For example; when they have a problem of hunger, floods, disaster or an outbreak of diseases or deaths, they get affected in one way or another and their behaviuors somehow change from the usual behaviuor you used to know.

Weapon 3

Understand Well your Responsibilities and Limits

After getting leadership, your first duty is to understand your job and its boundaries. If you were nominated or appointed, the appointing authority will provide you with appointment letter that will enumerate your duties, and to whom you will report to. The person you will report to is the limit to your authority. When you do work outside the outlined duties, you will find yourself interfering with other's authority or work, and those people whom you will have interfered with, will complain and even accuse you of interference to your boss.

For elected leaders, normally have no appointment letter, once they are announced the winners, they start work immediately. Their duties are mentioned in the constitution of the country, political party or even the relevant institution. Read carefully your duties and understand them. If there are areas you don't understand well, seek assistance from people who know them better or from the person who signed the letter.

On the other hand, there are other types of leadership which have no constitution or letters of appointment. For example, matrimonial partners or family members. In traditions and customs of many tribes in the country, a husband is the one who is the leader. Therefore, when you are pronounced a husband, immediately you are a leader of your wife and later of your children, in short, a leader of your family. However, all noted, your leadership of your family must have a limit/ boundaries. There are duties for a father, for a mother and children too. When you interfere with the duties of your spouse or children, they will complain and you may end up finding yourself being accused to your parents, or even clan head.

Any leader is not supposed to go beyond the boundaries of his /her duties. Do not interfere with the duties of other fellow leaders who are above or below you. When you do that, you will have initiated complaints, disputes or conflicts between you and your fellow leaders. When you are accused to the authority that appointed you, or party organs you will be found guilty and you will get despised by your fellow leaders or even disciplined. The weapon here is that, do not interfere with other people's duties, just do yours.

Weapon 4

Be Godly, Obey God's Commandments and your Religion's Teachings

It's very dangerous for people or members to be led by a leader who does not fear God, does not confess His presence and powers. Not only confessing His presence and powers, but, also must fear, love, praise, and worship Him. Be careful with a person who is seeking to be elected, but he/she does not worship Him. You must know that, a leader who does not fear God, will not respect you at all. Respect and obedience must start the with the Creator, the Almighty God and then will come to you.

A leader should obey God's commandments, instructions and teachings from his religion. However, if a contester cannot fulfill all the commandments, he should not be denied a position of leadership, because this is a result of his human weakness. For example; a christian who married a second wife or more, should not be denied political leadership or governmental leadership if at all he/she has got other good qualities. Such qualities are his/her ability to lead well. However, we shall not be surprised if he is refused leadership in his/her religion!

For certain, our country is not supposed to be led by leaders who do not fear, believe in and worship the Almighty God.

Weapon 5 

Keep Yourself Healthy by Preventing Yourself from Getting Ill Health

Health is the greatest asset (of all assets) to a human being. There is nothing more valuable than good health. Good health is life. After a person has become a leader, his/her good health becomes a big asset to the people he/she leads. They elected him/her or he was appointed in order to execute duties and to achieve certain specific goals. Without good health, his/her performance will be affected greatly depending on which type of disease. There are infectious diseases. There are diseases that arise from lifestyles, others depend on your behaviour, like diseases that are the outcome of sexual misconduct. There are diseases which are the outcome of you not observing health guidelines, like blood pressure, diabetes, heart diseases, amoeba etc. Also, there are diseases which are the outcome of bad, luck like cancers.

A leader is supposed to be seen caring for his/her health and taking precautions and measures of preventing infections. A leader must know the truth that when he/she gets sick, he will not serve well the people who elected him/her or those people whom he was given to lead. For this reason, he must be seen taking measures to prevent infectious diseases, diseases originating from bad lifestyles, diseases that are the outcome of not adhering to good principles of keeping good health, diseases of bad behaviours. Such steps include eating healthy foods, drinking moderately and doing physical exercises routively in order to prevent or manage high blood pressure, diabetes and heart diseases etc. Often do physical exercises, participate in games and sports and get enough time to rest your body and brain.

Respect the Retired Leaders

Retired leaders are those who were leaders before you in different posts/ positions of leadership. There is no leader who leads alone. Normally, there are different leaders who co-operate with you in leading. Those who came before you did that, and subsequent leaders will do that during their specific periods of time. Eventually, each one of them, at the right time retired, by deciding so himself, by not contesting again, by contesting and loosing or by not being appointed as a leader again. By any means, the end result is to leave leadership. Such leaders have retired from leadership. They may be living within or outside your area of your leadership. Some of them participated directly or indirectly, in campaining and electing or appointing you.

Some of them are older than you; they know better the area you are leading and its people more than you. They have got people who love them, who trusted them and those who gained a lot from their leadership. Those are not the people to ignore. Respect them, trust them, enthrone and use them to make your leadership a success. They are important people. Do not ignore them or do not fool yourself that their time has passed or that they are useless to your leadership. They are still there, use them. Go and visit them in their residences, listen to them, seek their advices on important issues in your area and take care of them, if you can, depending on your ability.

Visit and help them during their periods of sickness or bad health. Always remember that there will come a period when you will be like them and you will wish the leaders who will come after you to do the same to you.

Recognise and Respect Old People and Put Yourself in Their Hands

Old people are those with the age of sixty years and above. When years go beyond 85 (for some of them even less), some of those elders start losing some memory, their health continuous to deteriorate etc. These people deserve to be recognized, respected and cared for.

Old people are senior citizens of this country, they are nationalists who served this country for quite a long period of time, in politics, government, NGO's and Government organizations, in business, leadership, national defense, in delivering justice, in agriculture, animal husbandry, in fisheries etc. During their working periods, they contributed much to make this country what it is to-day. To you who are still continuing in service and leadership you have received the "race sticks" from them, in order for you to propel the country forward.

For sure, old people have huge experience and they have seen alot. They still have a reserve of experience and wisdom. They no longer lust for being leaders or executives. But, they have nationalism in them and love for their country. They are not jealous for your position.

You, as a leader, you need them. Recognize and respect them and their contributions to this country and put yourself in their hands so that they give you advice, they give you part of their experience, and pray for you to God and they will wish you all the best in your leadership.

Seek for their blessings and not their curses.

Your Should have Personal Advisers who are Educated, Competent, Experienced and knowlegeable in their Fields

We are used to hearing of the President's Advisers. The president appoints educated people, experienced and experts in their fields, who have national and international qualifications to be his/her advisers. Their big work is to help His Excellence the President not to make stupid mistakes when making decisions. A president's decision may either benefit the country or create problems. It is the citizens who will be greatly affected by his decisions. For this reason, the President is not supposed to or not even expected to make a mistake by acting or making a decision about anything without contacting his/her advisers for advice. However, the advice of every adviser should be based on technical analysis of the issue at hand, taking into accounts the factors of social, economy, politics, economics, diplomacy, signed national and international Agreements, laws etc.

However, advice is not necessary only for the president. Every leader has no permission of making stupid mistakes when making decisions. Actions and statements of any leader must be right, correct and well thought of. No leader is allowed to make stupid mistakes in decision making.

In order not to make such mistakes, he/she should get advice from people who can give him correct, informed and intelligent advices. Those advisers should be chosen by using different criteria, including their trust in you, their education and their experience in matters related to their responsibilities. It is advisable that every leader should have personal advisers. Their advices are in addition to the advices you may receive from official meetings and briefings from your personal staff. These advisers will enable you to lead well official meetings and to be seen by participants to meetings as an attentive a leader, with wisdom and vast experience.

What is important is that these advisers should not take the place of participants of meetings. Doing so would degrade the importance of the same and this may endanger your leadership or lead to misunderstandings between you and the participants to the meetings.

Weapon **9** 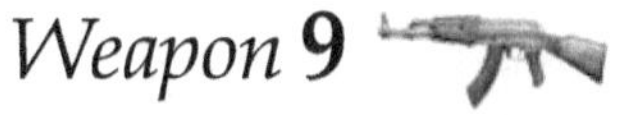

Do Not be an Unadvisable Person

One of the qualities of a good leader is that of being advisable. A good leader be advisable. Advice discussed here is not only that from personal advisers, discussed in Weapon number Eight. Even a ordinary citizen can advise you.

A leader may get advice by communicating with different groups within the locality he/she is leading. Such groups may be pupils, university students, youth, women, men, people with disabilities, campaigners for the conservation of the environment, politicians, farmers and fellow leaders.

All these people are intelligent and have their specific needs. Receive their advices, consider them, analyse them and take action on those you accept. Do not refuse advice of any kind. You nerver know, if you act on it, it may help you in your work and in your leadership.

In principle, advice is advice. Your are not obliged to believe in every advice you will be given. Some advices ae good and will - intentioned. On the other hand, there might be an advice which is not good at all. What is important is to receive it and analyse it. Then refuse the bad one and accept bad one good. Do not refuse any kind of advice which you have not analyzed. Should you do that, you will have made a big mistake, because you may have thrown out husks that contained rice (in them)?

Know the Importance of your Fellow Leaders

There is no leader who can lead a given locality alone. Even a husband does not lead his family alone. He co-operates with his wife and his children when they are mature. A husband is a leader, a wife is his deputy and children are assistants to both. Within a small village, street, village, county, constituency, district, region and nation, there are leaders of different kinds: political, governmental, religious, of co-operative unions, institutions, NGO's etc. All these work together in leading your area with the intention of bringing about development, solving disputes, complaints, problems etc.

You must recognise the importance of these leaders. They are important and they are your fellows. For this reason, respect each of them. Never despise any of them, do not neglect them, never interfere with their work and respect them in their presence and when they are absent. Besides not despising them, you should also not make them be despised in front of people.

Should there arise a misunderstanding between them and you or any of them, find an immediate solution. This will be for your benefit, your leadership and the citizens you lead.

Weapon **11**

Build and Strengthen Co-operation and Cohesion with your Fellow Leaders

Co-operation and cohesion between you and your fellow leaders is a necessity which you must build. Without co-operation and cohesion, there is no peace and development and there is no understanding between you. What is required is a united leadership. However, the latter does not come automatically, it must come from determined leaders, who desire to have it and who take actions to achieve that.

If you want to lead alone, you will not succeed. Luckily enough, in this country, at all levels of administration, there are different types of leaders and their number is big. Starting from the small village, village, ward, division, constituency, district, region and nation. At every level of administration, there are many leaders and of different kind: politicians, governmental, religious, traditional etc. You need to co-operate with all of them, not for your personal benefit only for the benefit of all the people you are leading.

When you do not do that, they will let you go alone, or you will lead alone, or they will not care for you at all. I am avoiding using the word "isolating" you because it is very strong, but it is there.

Take Good Care and Help Special Groups: People with Disabilities, Widows, People without help and Very old People

The groups mentioned above are everywhere in this country and in the world. They are there at every level of administration and leadership. It is important you know that in your area of leadership since they are there. What you are supposed to do is:

- To identify them.

- To help them be noticed by people who matter.

- To visit them and inquire about their conditions.

- To help them get proper medical treatment.

- To help them with whatever you can afford.

- To help them get employment.

- To request for donations for them from within and outside the country.

- To help them employ themselves.

- To pray for them to God.

- To show them that you care for them and you love them.

These groups have problems, sadness and special needs. They also need appropriate employment so that they can earn an income. There are many people in the society, who do not care for these people. You are not supposed to be one of them. Be different from them. When you care for them, God will bless you too. Also, when you love and respect them, they will respect you and love you too. Do not allow yourself to be blamed by such groups of people. Their prayers for you are heard by God and their thanks are sincere and come from the hearts.

Do not Rebuke, Despise or Threaten by mentioning in public, names of Workers, Executives and Fellow Leaders, Even if they Have made obvious Mistakes

Leaders, officers and executives are human beings. Every one of them has strengths and weaknesses. None of them is perfect. However, these are the people you have to work with and co-operate with them in your leadership. Without their co-operation, you will not deliver what you are expected of.

However, there are some weaknesses that are beyond tolerable level. Such weaknesses can be too much laziness, backbiting, poor services to people, receiving and giving bribes etc. Such weaknesses may be known to many people in that area. But, even if these weaknesses are known to many people, you as a leader, you are not supposed to blame them, to despise them and threaten them by mentioning their names in public and indoor meetings.

However, if you are an expert in using parables and sayings, you may do so without mentioning names of these people. What you may do is to inform their heads/bosses. If they are political leaders, inform leaders above them and if he/she is an appointed leader inform his/her boss or his/her appointing authority, and if he/she is an executive officer, inform the head of that department. Nowadays, the word "some" is often used and it saves you from direct blames. But, listeners will understand you and the targeted officer or officers will be happy that you did not mention their names and you did condemn them publically, but they will indeed get to know that you know their weaknesses and their mistakes. Those who were attentively listening to you will discover your wisdom and good judgment.

In so doing, you will have fulfilled your role without creating unnecessary friction between you and them and without lowering your respect. If you do the opposite of that, you will have lit fire that cannot easily be extinguished without yourself being burnt first. It's a mistake to burn yourself, and why should you do that?

In your office you have workers who assist you in executing your duties. Without them, your work efficiency will be affected. Also, there are workers in other offices which you cooperate with when discharging your duties and they know you and they understand your responsibilities. They have an opportunity of helping you or affecting your work performance.

These workers may be junior to you but they are very important people to you.

Respect and care these workers. If you do this, they will be very happy, they will love you, they will value you a lot and will portray your prestige, good qualities and image. The end result will be to work hard for you and with greater determination so as to make you continue succeeding in your leadership.

So, take good care of them, love them, respect them and value thier contributions to you and their work. They, in turn, will do the same to you and you will be happy.

Weapon **15**

Respect Resolutions made by Formal meetings even if you did not Participate in them

There are meetings which you are supposed to attend so that you can contribute your ideas. In these meetings, participants, including yourself, contribute ideas to every item of the agenda in order to reach decisions or resolutions. At the end of discussion on each item, the chairperson summaries what has been agreed upon. In doing so, normally he is guided by the principle of "majority carry the day". You might be or might not be one of the many. The rule of good governance requires you to accept and implement happily the decision reached by many in the meetings, even if you were opposing the particular item of the agenda.

To disagree to miss this rule is to one of the qualities of a good leader. Most of the time it happens, due to unavoidable circumstances, that you fail to attend meetings which you are a member. Your absence does not stop a meeting from making decisions so long as the quorum was available. Leadership rules of collective responsibility requires you to understand that you are part of the decisions that were made (although you were absent). You must respect them and supervise their implementation.

There are other meetings of which you are not a member, but they make decisions. Decisions of meetings are a result of different views and contributions made by majority or all the members of the meetings. You are obliged to be the first to respect those decisions. To disagree with them is to disrespect the majority. In order not to be judged as a person of such nature, you are expected to accept and to respect their decisions or resolutions.

In summary, one person is not a political party, government, a nongovernmental organization, company or institution. Majority of the participants of a meeting, are entiled to make resolutions which bind the institution, provided the said meetings were held as per their constitution, laws, by-laws or procedures governing such meetings. Because the decisions of the said meetings were made by the majority or all members present, they must be respected by every individual, especially, leaders including you.

You should not be Uncompromising on your Stand on Issues just because you see yourself as the only Person who is Right over Others

It is ignorance to see yourself as the only person who knows everything and who is right over others. You might excel other people in your locality in education, wealth, assets, experience etc, but, this does not make you a better person than others. You might have all these, but you do not have wisdom, good judgment or humanity. Besides, you may have all these, but you do not know well the environment you are in. You may know the environment, but, you don't know the history, traditions and customs of the people around.

It is because of this, that a good leader is one who listens and is a learner all his life. You should be ready to learn from others. Give your views, but, if you receive new information from a fellow member or members, feel free and happy to change your views or stand.

It is ignorance, and in fact you will be seen as an ignorant person, by insisting on your stand or your earlier views and to see yourself superior and more knowlegeable than of all other participants of the meeting, cheating yourself that you are the only one who is right.

Attend Meetings which you are a Member and present your Ideas

You are supposed to attend all meetings which you are a member, whether there are allowances to be paid or none. Your are a member because you were elected or you are an appointee of a certain authority. If you don't attend, you might affect the quorum, and this might lead to the meeting not being held. Or if it will be held, it will miss your ideas, views and contributions.

By not attending, the meeting might miss certain important information which might have changed the decision(s) reached (in your absence).

Because of these reasons, you are obliged to make every effort to attend all meetings which you are a member or you are an entitled participant. In these meetings, air you views, ideas and make suggestions which can help others make good and informed decisions. Speak and be heard. All the time do not forget that the people whom you lead follow and would like to know what you said in the meeting or whether you were asleep or you showed tiredness during the meeting you were attending.

Meetings are opportunities for participants to learn from each other and from the papers prepared for discussions. When a meeting is closed, and you were an active participant, you will realise that if you had not attended, you would have missed alot. So, please know that meetings are opportunities for gaining new knowledge, new information and new ideas. So, do attend.

Respect your Fellow Leaders

When you become a leader, you find other leaders in different levels of leadership and new others will join you as a leaders of your area of leadership. There are leaders in lower levels of administration or leadership and there are others in the upper levels of leadership than you and there are leaders who are at par or at the same level with you. All these expect you to respect them first and then they will also respect you. Do not expect to be respected by fellow leaders if you do not respect them. A senior leader should be the first to respect junior leaders who are young in age than you and who are in the lower levels of leadership.

Let you start and thereafter others will follow. Respect for a leader will be show itself in the following actions:

- To stand up when he comes to the place where you are.
- To clap your hands when he enters and leaves the meeting room/hall or when he makes an important or interesting point.
- Not to backbite him.
- Not to abuse him.
- Not to show him any sign of disrespect.
- Not to oppose or contradict him in public.
- To respect in public his statement or advice, even if you don't agree with him/her on what he said.
- To respect his family and associates.
- Not to correct him in public.
- If you don't agree with what he said in public or what he said was incorrect, correct him in privacy when you are two.
- To give him an important advice in privacy.
- Not to misguide, mislead or not to give him an incorrect advice etc.

Respect your Marriage and Love your Family First

A leader is a mirror to the people he leads. His actions are imitable. One of the pillars of a leader is his marriage and family. Even those leaders who are not allowed to marry and raise families, they have "their types of marriage and families." Examples of such leaders are priests of the Catholic Church. Their marriage is their priesthood and their families are the believers under their leadership.

Some of the leaders, especially, politicians, have shaky marriages. One of the reasons for this situation is lack of enough time to stay with their matrimonial partners and their children. This is not a secret. During the period they are not together, some of the husbands and some wives behave in the ways not acceptable to married people. Satan is certainly at work. The result is a shake marriage and lose respect from the society, friends and relatives. Eventually some of such marriages end up in separation or divorce. Their children are adversely affected.

However, there are many politicians who have united, strong and happy marriages. This being the result of commitment of the matrimonial spouses to make their marriage strong and happy. The secret behind this is prayers to God, seeking assistance, being faithful to each other, living a moderate life and tolerance to each other. A leader not to have a good marriage is a very bad thing. Also, a leader to marry or be remarried often is not a good reputation.

Besides, a leader to have a problematic marriage is not good example to the people he leads. On the other hand, a leader to have no marriage is not a mistake. Also, a leader to have not yet married or to have not been married is not a mistake, neither is this a disqualification for being a leader.

In life, to be married is good, but to have a happy marriage is the most important and most rewarding achievement. I appeal and advise you, leader, to respect and love your marriage and keep it that way for life. Love your spouse and children. In short, love your family. Besides, respect other peoples' marriages. Remember that a leader has a period of leadership and that period will one day end, but, your marriage lasts longer than your leadership period. The marriage is supposed to last till death separates you. Your children are the outcome of your marriage and together you constitute a family. Love and keep intact the latter. Leaders who have good marriages are lucky and happy in two main ways: firstly, they have happiness which originate from the very marriage including having children (if they were lucky to bear children) and secondly, they have happiness resulting from the leadership.

Let me emphasise: normally, a marriage produces children. Parents and their children form a family. You, as a leader, you are more respected by having a family. Take great care of and respect it. Your children are the matrimonial products, parents and leaders of tomorrow. Their parents are their foundation school, preparing them for forthcoming responsibilities in fostering families and national development.

Weapon **20**

Respect the Constitution and Laws of the country so that you become a Good citizen

A leader should be a good example to the people he leads by understanding and respecting the country's constitution and laws. The main purpose of doing so is to be an exemplary leader and citizen. Never do actions and make statements which can land you into trouble and end up in the police custody and courts of law. This is not befitting you as a leader.

One of your duties is to educate the people you lead to know well, obey and respect the constitution and laws of their country. The people you lead should be good citizens and not the opposite and you should be their role model.

Leaders who have no respect for the consitution of their country and who often disobey the laws and consequently often end up in police custody and in the courts of law ashame the people they lead and should not continue leading.

You should strive not to be one of them. You should aim at being a role model for the people you lead.

Separate your Leadership from your Egoism

Before you become a leader you were yourself. After being a leader you have another title bestowed on you, that's a leadership. So, there are two entities in you: yourself (egoism) and (your) leadership. There are things which don't concern yourself although they affect your leadership.

I know that it is a bit difficult to separate these two entities, but, they must be separated. People must see that you have separated them.

Learn to put on the hat of leadership when you are executing leadership functions and put on the hat of yourself when you are acting as an individual or yourself. People must see that you are good at wearing the two hats at appropriate occasions.

To elaborate this point, let me use an example of a military officer. During office hours, he puts on military uniform, but when he returns to his home, he immediately removes the uniform and puts on civilian dress and people who don't know that he is a military officer and find him at his home in civilian attire will not immediately know that he is a military officer. Although is in this way he has managed to know when to separate the two hats!

In the same way, you should be an expert at separating your leadership from your egoism. It is easy. Practise it and do it. Your people will love it.

Do not Accept an Advice from your Advisers which you do not Believe being Correct

A leader to have advisers is not questionable. Different leaders have advisers, even yourself should have an adviser or advisers. Their role is to advise you only. Your advisers should be conversant and expert in the issues they advise you. They should have learnt them at higher institutions of learning and have vast experience and exposure. They must be knowledgeable. But, their advice remains an advice. It is not an order to you. You are not obliged to believe and accept them all as correct. Together with the advice you may get by way of mouth or in writing from them, use also your intelligence, experience and exposure to the issue at hand, to arrive at a right decision. Always, weigh the advices you receive. You will be a laughable leader if you accept every advice you receive from your advisers and use it to make decisions.

Always remember that it may happen that one or more of your advisers may be on the payroll of your enemies or opposers and they use them to bring you down. Because of this, always be careful with advices you receive from your advisers and don't accept every advice as being correct or well intentioned. Also, it is advisable that you should find enough time to consider carefully every advice you receive. For an example an advice might be correct economically at the material time, but, it might bring you trouble politically.

Remember that advices are necessary to you but always bear in mind that not all advices you receive are well researched and not all advices are well intentioned. Take great caution on advisers as some of them might be on the payroll of your enemies and their main role is to destroy and bring you down from your position.

Weapon **23**

Be Creative, Liberationist and with
New Ideas in order to move Forward

A leader must be creative, strategic, a champion for others' rights and endowed with new ideas in order for his/ her to move people forward. It is not good for you always to be an implementer of strategies. Where are yours? How and what is going to be your legacy? On what will you be remembered, or praised for?

But, you cannot be so if you do not read books, newspapers, visit the internet and social media, watch TV and listen to radios. You cannot be such a leader if you do not attend indoor and open meetings, seminars, workshops, conferences, symposia etc. You cannot be so if you lock yourself into your house, without visiting other leaders and places, like wards, constituencies, districts, regions, provinces and countries others than the place you lead.

This is because new education, new ideas, new strategies etc can be learned outside the box. Do not confine yourself into your own box! If you don't do that, the place you lead will remain backward, compared to neighbouring places lead by fellow leaders at the same level of leadership, but, are more visionary and daring than you. They have opened their boxes in search of new knowledge and ideas for the betterment of the places they lead.

Love, Take care and Respect People

It is people who gave you leadership through their votes or you were appointed to lead and to serve them, in order for them, to develop, to advance in their religious belief, or make step forward in different areas of development, such as economic, social etc.

So, you, being their leader, have one main purpose, that's to serve them. You are their servant. You are their representative. You are their mirror. You are their voice.

For this reason, without them you have no leadership, even if you will continue to be called their leader till when the period of your leadership ends. To you, the most important resource is the people you lead. In order to be happy with your leadership and be a successful one, you must:

- Love the people you lead.
- Take great care of them.
- Respect them.
- Be courteous to them.
- Eat and drink with them.
- Be happy with them.
- When they are in difficulties, be with them and show sympathy and be of assistance to them.
- Participate in mourning's of their beloved ones.
- Bury the dead.
- Prove yourself to them that really you are one of them etc.

Do not Harbour Hatred with People

Hatred is the behaviuor of disliking people or having no love for people or resentment. So, a person with hatred is a person with resentment, bitterness or animonisity towards people.

To a leader, hatred is very bad. You are not expected to have hatred with any person or a group of people, even if they have annoyed you. You might have been annoyed, but, do not show them your annoyance in anyway. Just swallow it.

Remember that hatred breeds hatred. Eventually your leadership will be affected. Do not wear hatred. Be afraid of hatred. The opposite of hatred is love. So, love your people.

Weapon **26**

Believe in Equality and Universal Brotherhood with all Human Beings

See all human beings as your brothers and sisters. You are also a human being. All of us are the descendants of Adam and Eve. We are all the creatures of God and were created equally. Our basic needs are the same. These needs are food, shelter, medical care and education. We may be distinguished by gender, colour, nationality, faith or good education, wealth etc, but, all these don't disqualify us from being brothers and sisters.

As a leader, you must believe in earnest in Equality, Brotherhood and Sisterhood. Never discriminate a person for any reason, be it gender, colour, nationality, faith (religion), tribe, education or the amount of wealth one possesses.

What is important is that we were all created equal and in the image of God. Before God we are all equal. Our task and duty is to prove to each other that we are equal and we have common and basic needs.

Do not Pass by People without Greeting them or at least Waving at them

You are the leader of a people, people you love and respect. It is these people who enabled you by their votes to have the respect you now have. It is these people who enabled you to receive your salary, allowance and other amenities.

Because of their importance to you, do not pass them on the road or any gathering without stopping to greet them or at least waving at them, or stopping to talk or address them even if it is for a short period.

Also, never close windows of the vehicle you are using if you pass through places with clouds of people. If you do so, they will shut you out by removing you from leadership, or they will cause you to be removed from leading them by your appointing authority. They will accuse you of arrogance, disrespect, despising them and seeing yourself better than them.

Remember that by doing so will cost you less, but, by not doing so will cost you millions of dolloars (money).

Love and Respect Children, Youths and Women

I am not discriminating men. To the contrary, they deserve the respect they deserve. But, women deserve special respect. Every person knows the importance of women. Without their special powers, we would not see children, no husbands, no families, no nations and no development of any kind on earth. Women are hard workers. They take great care of children, families and are the best nurses in the world. The children grow and become adults.

On the other hand, children and the youths are tomorrow's parents, workers and leaders. They are the inheritors of the present parents and leaders.

Visit, view TVs, Youtube, attendances of the over 2,400 Christian sets, Muslim sects, and other denominations, political campaigns and you notice that over 60% are women and children in attendance and participation in different groupings. The men occupy the remains 40%. Religious leaders at all levels of leadership see this situation and note it!

It is these three groups (children, youth, and women) who influence the results in the elections of all types or appointments of leaders.

For this reason, these three groups are very important to you, your leadership and to the development of your area under your leadership. So, love them, recognize them because their importance and respect them, then they will do the same to you.

Listen to the People you lead so that you Learn How they See you and What they Say about you

If you want to be a good leader, you have to be a good listener. You must not be a person in hurry. Listen to the people you lead, one by one, in a group of more than one in public and indoor meetings. Often ask some people (not relatives and friends) how people see you and what they say about you. Do not be afraid of people talking about you positively and negatively. Do not be afraid of different remarks and opinions about you made by different people. All the times you should know that you are not perfect. You have weaknesses, as any human being has, some big and others small. It is better if people see them and would like you to get rid of them or seeing you making great effort to get rid of them all or to reduce them and never repeat them. It is by doing so that people you lead will love you, will see you as a courageous person, and a leader who is able to correct himself/herself after realizing his/her mistakes or weaknesses.

Speak for the People you lead Without Fear of Anybody

A people's leader is one who is sympathetic, committed and and who is close to them. For this reason, he is supposed to speak for them and to fight for them, without fear of anybody, against exploitation, oppression and denial of their rights. You must be seen doing that and they must see you doing whatever possible to get lid of these vices. You should not be part of them.

You should not be afraid of anybody, whether he/she is a leader or an executive officer if he is acting against the laws and norms. I know they will hate you and they will even denigrate you, do not care. Your defender is the people you lead. They will always be on your side, shoulder to shoulder with you. You will receive your reward in the love and support they give you. Don't fear, move forward. As a leader you are expected to be strong on basic issues and principles like these, be it night or day time.

Fight for Peace and Development of your People

Peace is freedom from disturbance. Peace is when there is tranquility, calmness or no war. On the other hand, development is progress socially, economically and politically. In order to get development, there must prevail peace. Without peace among the people you lead, there will be no development because people cannot work. There is no peace where there is war, hatred, disturbances, misunderstandings etc.

Because of this, you must be seen fighting for the presence of peace. The existence of peace is the result of existence of calmness, good understanding between people, cooperation and togetherness between the people you lead and between them and their neighbours. Never should you encourage the disappearance of peace because if the latter is lost, it will be very hard to restore it, and without peace there is no development.

After attaining peace, push for development in all spheres, including education, economy, social, political, cultural etc. But, remember that development is the result of working hard diligently, use of science and technology and discipline. Lazy people and those who prefer to be idle should be helped to change, including taking legal measures against them.

Weapon 32

You must be an Advocate of Justice

You must come out openly as a lover and fighter for the rights of the people you lead. Every person is looking for his/her rights. There is no person who does not want to be given his/her rights, but, many miss it. They are deprived of it without their will.

Champion the rights of all your people, without discrimination of age, gender, colour, faith, tribe, nationality, their origin etc. The rights I am talking about here include the rights of children, women, the disadvantaged groups, old people, the right to chose a religion and all other rights mentioned in the national constitution and UN Human Rights Declaration.

Respect your Time and the Time of Other People

Time is an important and scarce resource to you and other people. Time is a scarce resource to all people. A day has 24 hours. In our country, out of these only 12 hours are available for work. Out of these 12, really the period of work is between 7.0 am and 4.0 pm, that is 10 hours. Therefore, to take away any time during this period of working of 10 hours is to deprive them of their time they should have used to produce goods or provide services to others.

Because of the importance of time, you should not aim at taking more of their time which they use in production and provision of services. Spend as short a time as is possible. To achieve this, if you plan to meet them in a public or indoor meeting, be in time as announced earlier and be brief in your address.

On the other hand, officers who arrange your meetings should tell the people the exact time of your arrival and the exact time of starting the meeting. If the leader will arrive at 11.0 am, the people must be told so and not one or two hours earlier as is being done to-day by some officers in the districts, wards and villages.

People to wait for the arrival of a leader for more than half-hour is to waste the resourceful time and it is disrespect to them. On the other hand, a leader who is strict with time of arrival for meetings is respected by the people and officers who arrange his/her meetings.

Estimate correctly the time needed to arrive at the venue of the meeting so that you leave in time your office, home, hotel or the proceeding meeting place. If you respect time, time will build up your respect.

On the other hand, respecting time is not for public meetings only, it must be so for every occasion: be it for appointments with other leaders, officers, place of worship, business, official, private etc. Always respect and keep appointment time. A religious leader who starts the service in the time and minds the time of worshippers is respected very much. A person who does not respect time of others is disrespected. Mwalimu Julius K. Nyerere, the First President of Tanzania and the Father of the Nation was known to keep time and was also respected for this. Also, Parliament is known to keep time. At exactly 9.0 am the opening prayer starts.

Be Hardworking and Disciplined at Work

A leader is a worker or a farmer. You must do your work diligently and be disciplined. Besides, you must use current knowledge in executing your work. A lazy person who has no discipline and who does not use current knowledge is not suitable to be a leader. He is not suitable because all the time a leader should be a role model for his people.

There is always work to be done, whether it is in the office, field, farm, livestock keeping, in non-governmental organisations, sports, recreation activities etc. Do not say that there is no work to be done. There will always be work to be done. However, whatever type of work you do, do it deligently and with discipline.

Hate Corruption, because it is the Enemy of Justice and Peace. Do not receive it or Give it to Anyone

Corruption is the enemy of Justice. If there is no Justice, there is no Peace. Because of this, hate it. Do not receive it or give it in exchange of your rights or rights of other people. Corruption buys the rights of a person. Defend your people against any type of corruption. Educate your people on the negative effects of corruption. Shout at people who give corruption. Shout at people who demand corruption. Be a good example by refusing to receive or demand corruption. This must include the period leading to election or/and appointment time.

There are many types of corruption: sexual, material and other types. Corruption can be small, medium and grand. All are corruptions although they differ in scale, magnitude and effects.

You should not do Fornication and Adultery

An act of sexual intercourse between two persons of different sexes has different interpretations. If it is between two persons married according to the tradition, government or religions, with the acceptance of the parents, brothers and sisters and relatives of both sides, it is called **"act of marriage"** or **marriage.** But, if it is between two persons of different sexes, but, not done according to the above procedures, that is, not married officially, it is called **fornication** or **adultery.**

Fornication is a sexual act done by a person of one sex who is not married with a person of a different sex who is not married (to a woman or man).

Adultery, on the other hand is a sexual act between a married or unmarried person of one sex with a married person of another sex or vice versa. In this latter relationship, there will be a person who will be hurt or deprived of his or her right.

Sex between two formally married persons of different sexes is called marriage, is rightful and must be respected by all people. Fornication and adultery are immoral and have no respect in them and in society. They must be condemned by all people who are moral.

But, in fact the act is the same. The only difference is that marriage is blessed and permitted, while fornication and adultery is prohibited by all customs and traditions, all Books (the Quran and Bible) and is one of the Ten Commandments of God handed over to Prophet Musa on Mount Sinai.

However, this commandment is often broken by believers and non believers. It is broken by married people and non married people. It is broken by even some of our religious leaders (junior and senior) including some of those who swore not to marry in life, that's not to marry or be married in their lives, in short, celibacy.

Different categories of leaders: politicians, junior and senior government officers, chief executives and officers of public and private institutions and companies etc are often alleged to commit these acts. However, these vices are not confined to this country only. They are found in all countries of the world, including USA, Europe, China, Asia, Africa etc. If is often heard that a certain Minister in some of these countries has resigned because he has be discovered doing that and does not want to remain in the government as he would dainty it.

To be called an adulterer or a fornicator is not a respect. It is a sin and an act of shame to you and to your matrimonial partner, your children, your fellow leaders, your religious leaders, parents, guardians etc.

But, it is a popular act performed by many people, without regard to gender, tribe, nationality, social position, whether married or not, leadership position etc.

Despite all this, adultery and fornication remain shameful acts and dangerous. These two vices have contributed greatly to the weakening or breaking up of many marriages, quarrels, fights, deaths, hatred among neighbours, friends, brothers and sisters and have contributed a lot to infections and spread of sexual diseases, including HIV/AIDS, resignations and removal of people from positions of leadership and falling short of good leadership qualities.

Once you are a leader, you must deny yourself of a good thing, so sweet, which you can afford financially or otherwise, which can land you into trouble or cause you problems. Adultery and fornication are not for you as they will earn you disrespect from the society, clan members, family members, your matrimonial partner, and may break up your marriage or lose your leadership or not be re-elected or re-appointed next time. My advice to you is to refrain from these two vices. You lose nothing by doing so.

Weapon **37**

You should not be Homosexual

Homosexuality is the act of two persons of the same sex (whether intercourse or outcourse). Gayness is for two men and lesbianism is for two women. The two are shameful acts and do not please God. They are sins and forbidden in the Holy Bible and Holy Quran. Also, our traditions, cultures and norms do not allow these acts. Even laws of many countries including ours forbid them. Gay in Kiswahili means *hanithi, msenge, basha*. People who practice it are called *Mashoga*. Lesbian in Kiswahili is called *Msagaji*.

If these acts are done by a leader, they affect adversely his/her reputation. Whether he is a political leader, a religious leader, a family leader, a government leader etc., the people he leads despise him and affects their belief. If a family leader has this behaviour, family members are disrespected in the eyes of other people who also despise him. In many countries, if a political leader, government leader, religions leader etc is a gay or lesbian he/she is despised by people he leads and fear him.

They suspect him that he/she might spoil their children or the youths of both genders, pupils/students, their wives or their husbands. They see him/her as evil person who has no good manners. He/she is regarded as a dangerous person to their marriages and children.

A leader of this type looses the moral authority and enthusiasm to speak against these social evils in the society. Farther, he cannot encourage his/her people to refrain from doing actions which might lead to infection of sexual diseases, which include HIV/AIDS. Hence, I appeal to you leader not to be classified as a gay or lesbian. It is against the good manners, the ethics of leadership and good governance in this country.

40

Weapon **38**

You should Not be a Drunkard

Drinking alcohol moderately as a way of refreshing oneself is not bad, unless forbid by one's religion. What is not permitted is drinking alcohol excessively, till one becomes drunk. Drunkardness of any extent is not permissible for a leader. Drunkardness reduces the respect of a leader. Drunkardness makes a leader utter words or statements which he is not expected to utter or might lead him to do certain unwelcome actions which otherwise he/she would not do when sober, or shameful actions, dangerous statements or do actions which are against the law. For certain, drunkardness is not good for any person, especially, a leader. Also, alcohol affects the nerves of a person and other organs etc. this results in bad health or his/her death.

You are allowed to drink moderately, but, not drinking till you are drunk.

Weapon **39**

Do not use your Wealth to buy People, Voters, Journalists and Other Media people

A leader to be rich is not bad. What is bad is to use your wealth to "buy" people, to corrupt voters in order to vote you into power and to corrupt journalists to write good things only and publish them in the newspapers, and media people to broadcast them in the TVs, radios and other electronic media. This will make you be elected and continue leading people even if you have lost the good qualities to continue leading them.

You will be their leader, but, even yourself know that you are no longer fit to continue leading them this term. Because of this, you will let them down developmentwise and in the quest for their rights and when you relinquish leadership because of any reason, they will hate you for a long period to come and will spit on you.

Weapon **40**

You should Not be a Beggar or Loafer

A beggar is a person who lives by begging, by asking others for money, food etc. On the other hand, a **loafer** is a person who is an idler and wastes other peoples' time instead of working.

It is not good for a leader to be either a beggar or a loafer. Hence, you should have gainful work to do or be employed or employ yourself, that will generate you income. Such employment can be crop, livestock and fish farming, beekeeping, poultry keeping, self employment, business etc.

It is not good for you to be known to move from home to home, place to place or going to individuals you lead begging for money, food or anything else. It is not good for you to be seen a beggar or loafer. If you do that, you will have no respect in the society and you will be despised. Never be a beggar or a loafer.

Weapon **41**

Do not Praise Yourself even if you Deserve it

Praise is given to a person or persons by another person or other persons. A leader should not praise himself/herself publicly. Your duty is to work had for their development and be well mannered. These two attributes will make people you lead accord you praise. Never praise yourself in front of a person or persons. Do not call yourself "Honourable." Do not tell people that you are very intelligent, that you are hospitable, that you are a very good person etc.

To praise yourself is equivalent to glorify oneself, by seeing yourself to be better than other people. This is not good character and you should not do that.

Weapon **42**

You should not Build a Wall between You and the People you lead

Never build a wall or place a curtain between you and your people. If you do that, how will you see them or hear them? I advise you that your office and home should be open to your people all the time. All your telephone or mobile numbers should be known to them and never close them or be uncharged. All the time you should be reachable. For a leader, even on the road or path, you can listen to people with different reasons wanting to talk to you: some of them might have problems of different sorts, need your assistance or have an advice for you. Never tell them to come tomorrow. Listen to them on the spot and make decisions immediately.

A leader has no night or day time which he/she has no work. All the time you are at work. Your phone can ring even at midnight. If it rings pick it up and take action immediately. A leader does not close his/her phone at night just because he wants peace and no disturbance when he is asleep. You must remember that you are a servant of your people for 24 hours per day.

You Should Not Be Revengeful

Revenge is an act of doing something evil to someone who hurt you or acted inhumanly or unjustly to you in the past. Being a leader, you are not expected to revenge. If you do that, then, you are not a leader. To be annoyed by someone, to be corrected openly, to be despised unjustly, to be abused, to be insinuated, to be written or reported negatively in the print and electronic media etc are common to a leader.

You will revenge to how many people? For sure, there are many! Instead, what you can do is to refute the allegations or to keep silent or to close your eyes and ears or to correct yourself.

That is good leadership.

Weapon **44**

Do Research, be Careful and Always Talk Sense

A leader must always be careful with what comes out of his/her mouth: his statements, spoken words and actions. You should not be loose-tongue. Always aim at talking less and sense. Always do your own research on any issue before you pronounce it or take action on it. Analyse the issue at hand. Get advice from people you believe can give you correct and good advice, people who have good ideas, positive people, people you believe wish you good only and people who can give you professional advices.

After that, then make your decision or make known to people your stand on the issue. As a leader you should not be loose-tongue, uttering words and statements on issues before you make a thorough research. Make sure that always you do not talk nonsense and you should not pervert or mislead issues or people.

Always remember the wise statement of the Great Leader of China, Mao Tse Tung, that "without research you have no right to speak." It is very dangerous for any leader not to be careful or be a talker of nonsense or be a misleader of truth.

Prepare Yourself Well for Meetings

If you have arranged to meet one or more persons, or if a meeting has been arranged for you by your assistants or fellow leaders to meet a person or people, prepare yourself well for the same. Make sure your body is clean; the dress should much your title, age, sex, event, season and time. Prepare yourself well on the subject(s) before you and how you will talk or present your views. Do proper research on the issues for the meeting. It is even better to do a rehearsal. Remember that all good international and national speakers prepare themselves well, write speeches or notes and do rehearsals.

If you are a C.E.O. of a company or an institution, make sure that your assistants have prepared for you written dossiers, speeches, have analysized the issues and make to you recommendations and have made themselves available for you to discuss with them what they have prepared. The main reason of holding discussions with them is to have a clear understanding of their recommendation and for you to make known to them also your views on their recommendations. The same applies to political and government leaders.

Your physical appearance, personality, business-like, seriousness, sense of humour are very important at meetings because they help you win the people attending the same to your side. It does not matter whether the meetings involves people you lead or people from outside of your area of leadership.

Let me emphasize that, it is very important to prepare yourself on issues you will talk about. Your preparations can be a written summary or a written speech. Whatever will come out of your mouth must have been researched on, correct and not confusing. You should always talk sense and appear to the people to be knowledgeable and learned.

You must be sure and correct on what you will say in the meetings and be able to defend them with statistics and authentic documents.

Another way of preparing yourself is your posture, how you will sit or stand up while addressing the meeting, what type of dress you will be putting on, what type of shoes, spectacles etc.

Also, how your voice should be heard. In your speech, is there a place to laugh, to be angry, to be happy, to clap, to show unhappiness or displeasure about something etc. How will you greet the people attending the meeting and how will you bid them farewell? Regarding the meeting procedure: will you start by listening to them or fellow leaders or will you start immediately addressing them and will you say all or part of what you had prepared?

Will you allow the people to ask questions, give you their opinions, advices etc or not. Have you prepared your fellow leaders, your assistants or executives to answer some of the questions which come under their responsibilities or not. In short, prepare yourself well when going to meet and address people or when going to attend any meeting or whenever you are going to meet one or more persons.

In these days, remember that you are being recorded using their mobile phones without your permission and knowledge!

Weapon **46**

Do not be a Hypocrite, a Fickle person and a Giver of unlimited Promises

A hypocrite is a person who pretends to have certain opinions or high moral standards, when this is not really true. A hypocrite says the opposite of his/her actions. A hypocrite is a person who promises but does not implement the same.

A leader must be principled and have firm stands on issues. If you say or promise something, you have to implement the same. Always remember that whatever you utter is highly respected and believed by the people you lead.

Once you have said it, it is said. Once you promise, you have made a promise. What is needed is to be careful with what you say or promise. Don't say or promise something which you cannot honour. If you are forced to say something, say such words like, "I will see," "I shall consider it," "I shall work on the issue," "I shall take it to higher authorities," "I shall try," etc. Fear being called a fickle person or a giver of many promises that you cannot implement or honour. In short, you should not be a hypocrite or a fickle person or a giver of unlimited promises or promises that you cannot implement.

Weapon **47**

You Should be Truthful and Transparent in Your Life

As a leader you must always be truthful and transparent. People will despise you if you are not so. A truthful person is free in this world. He/she has nothing to hide. This truth will give you freedom. A transparent person is not meanness. He/she has nothing to hide in his everyday life. If you offend him/her, he/she will tell you immediately his/her feelings so that you can correct yourself and everything ends there.

People have no grain of doubt on the truthful and transparent leader, because his/her behaviour and actions are well known to them.

You Should not Owe Money to Individuals

A leader should not owe money to individuals. Let you be demanded by banks and other financial institutions, but not individuals. Do not forget the saying, "borrowing is happiness, but, paying a loan is a mourning." If people you lead start demanding you for unpaid loans, they will spread bad news on you and this will affect you negatively and your respect will diminish.

One morning you may wake up and find many people at your gate or door steps demanding payments of their unpaid loans. What will you do? Will you open the gate or door of your house and face them, especially, if you have no money? Or will you hide yourself in the house and instruct people you live with in the house to tell them that you are not in the house, that you went for a safari, while actually you are in the house! What about if they start stonning the house or set it on fire, will you continue hiding in the house or you will be forced to come out in shame.

The media people will come to record the whole incident and report the same. If this happens, will your seat be safe next election or if you are an appointee, will you retain the post? Take great care of this weapon.

Weapon **49**

Be Careful with Some of Your Friends

Do not believe that all your friends are good to you. If you investigate, or do some research, you will realize that some of your friends do evil actions in the society, like adultery, armed robbery, drink excessively, sell and use outlawed drugs etc. Experts have sayings that "if you want to know the behaviour of a person, look at the behaviors of his/her friends." For this reason, if you don't be careful with some of your friends, you might be associated with their evil actions. This is because people will ask, "How can he/she be a friend of this armed robberer if he/she is not an armed robberer?

For this reason, select friends with whom to continue friendship with. Once you are a leader, leave those friends who are accused or suspected of doing evil actions in society. If you do so, people will understand you well and will forgive you for your past friendship with them. People must be satisfied that your friendship with them has ceased completely and not that you are cheating them.

On the other hands, some of your friends may appear good people in front of you, but in your absence say and do bad things against you. They might be associated with your enemies and provide the latter with inside information on you which they have acquired because of your friendship with them. For sure, not all your friends are good to you. For this reasons do not trust all your friends.

Respect all 'Modern' Religions, their Leaders and Worshippers of Traditional Religions

The country's constitution allows a citizen to join any religion he prefers. Because of this constitutional right, you lead people who worship God vide many 'modern' religions. You also lead worshippers of traditional religions. Respect all religions, their followers and leaders. It is not your duty to choose a religion for any of them.

It is mandatory to respect leaders of all religions, without favourtism to some of them. This is because together, they lead the same people you lead. It is not you who elected or appointed them, and the weaknesses of some of them should not bother you. Cooperate with them to conceive of and supervise implementation of development projects in the area of your leadership. Further, work together with them (religious leaders) so that development can come to your area. Cooperate with them to fight poverty and to remove all development obstacles and people's complaints. Cooperate with them to eliminate injustices and exploitation in society. Cooperate with them to fight small, big and grand corruption and bureaucracy.

Weapon **51**

You must be a True Democrat

You must be seen to respect and believe in the principles of democracy. Instill this belief of yours in the people you lead. People must believe in the democracy and its advantages.

People must participate in different elections and stand to be elected in different positions of leadership. People must be educated on how to elect good and able leaders. People should refuse being corrupted during the process leading to nomination and during the actual voting day.

People must know that democracy will make their freedom last, so is their humanity.

Love and Participate in Sports and Body exercises

You are advised to love and participate in sports and body exercises. These two help maintain good health, friendship, cooperation and happiness among people. Encourage and help your people to love and participate in sports and body exercises.

They should build grounds for both traditional and modern sports

These sports and exercises should be done by both genders and all ages: children, youths, pupils, students in all learning institutions, adults, disabled people and the old people. All these groups will benefit from doing so.

Weapon **53**

You should be Humble but Not Simpleton

It is important to be humble, but not simpleton. A humble person is one who lowers himself than he actually is, it is a big person who lets himself to be like a small person. Simpleton is an unintelligent person who can be easily tricked. You should not lower yourself to that level. if you are humble, people will love you and will elevate you to the level you deserve.

To be humble does not mean that you are a simpleton. In other words, your humbleness should not be too much as you can be classified as a simpleton.

Weapon **54**

Educate Yourself in order to have Enough education

The words "enough education" might raise confusion and different meanings or interpretations, this is because it depends on where you are and time. But, what is obvious, is that, the time when people were lead by people who did not know how to write and read is gone. At present each Ward has one or more secondary schools. Education at primary level has been improved. Every school age child should be in school and should pass final primary level exams. The nation's aim is to make every citizen in the country literate. At present, to have a Form IV education is common. Besides, every year thousands of people graduate from Colleges, Institutes and Universities with Diplomas, First, Masters and PhD degrees. These days, retired officers are on the increase in sub-villages, villages and streets.

In these circumstances, if you don't have enough education, you will not be able to lead educated people comfortably. They will flood you with questions which you might not be able to answer with ease and they will not stop gossiping on you.

For this reason, if you think your education is low, you should make special effort to improve it through different means, such as, enrolling in evening classes, seminars, workshops, short courses etc.

Besides, daily listen to radios and watch different TV stations within and outside the country, cultivate the habit of reading books, newspapers, magazines and visit the electronic media. For sure, a leader who reads books and other print media will prove to be an intellectual and knowledgeable. I advise you to be such a leader.

Weapon 55

Encourage your People to Educate themselves to their Ability and to Use it to Benefit all People

By realizing the importance and contribution of education in changing people in order to develop, encourage them to educate themselves by reading books, magazines and newspapers, to watch TV stations, to listen to radios, to attend meetings, conferences, seminars, workshops and discussions.

Learning is a lifelong activity. They must educate themselves up to their ability. The slogan of each of them should be, "I shall educate myself to the level of my ability and to use my education for benefit of all people." In order to realize this slogan, encourage construction and establishment of Libraries and Learning Centres up to Sub-villages and streets.

Encourage Expansion and improvement of Education in your Area

By recognizing the importance of education to the development and raising the standard of living of an individual, his/her family, sub-villages; streets, villages, wards, divisions, districts, regions and country, encourage and motivate your people to expand and participate in the improvement of education from the levels of Nursery, Primary, Secondary, Technical Institutes up to University level.

Investment in education should be given priority. It is education, in particular good education, that will revolutionise our agriculture and the economy of the country etc. Without your people being educated, at least up to secondary level, do not expect fast development. For this reason, encourage and motivate your people to give to their children good education their top priority.

Weapon **57**

Be a Role Model Leader in All Aspects of Life

You should strive to be a role model in every aspect for your people. These aspects can be good habits, good manners, excellent leadership, diligence at work, displine, educating you etc.

Remember that people learn from their leaders. If you are a bad example in the above aspects, some people, especially the youth, might imitate you, and that will be too bad.

A leader with bad manners is a liability and a shame to himself, his family members, to the area he leads and to the nation.

For this reasons a leader must always be a Role Model in all aspects of life to his people.

Never be the opposite.

Weapon **58**

Respect, Love and Cooperate with your Neighbours

Where you live, where you have your office, your shop etc. there are neighbours. The latter are very important to you. They know well how you live with people. They know how you live with your spouse. They know how you live and take care of your children. In short they know you well. They also know well your wife/husband and children. For this reason they can build your good image or destroy it.

Because of this, respect them, love them and cooperate with them in all issues, incidents and occasions of happiness and sadness, bury the dead, give out condolences, sleep with them during mourning periods for the dead, participate with them in ending the mourning periods of their beloved ones, live well with them etc.

It is extremely important to do so in order for them to do the same for you.

If you are Able, Make Contributions and Grants to the Needy

If you are able, give contributions and grants to poor people and contribute money and/or goods for the development of your area. If you don't do so, while you have the ability, people will call you several nick names including "thrift," "miser" etc.

The words, "if you are able" must be noted with caution, so that you do not overdo it to the extent of affecting the welfare of your family.

Weapon **60**

Respect the Media and their Employees

The media can build or destroy you. They can punish you or help you make a success of your leadership. For this reason, the media organs, their owners and their employees are very important to your leadership. These organs include radios, televisions, newspapers, blogs etc. The role of these organs include dissemination of news, educating and entertaining people. The role of the media is of topmost importance, difficulty and dangerous.

Recognize this role, respect and value them and their employees, but, never "buy" them and never corrupt their employees so that they even write what is not correct or right, in order to protect you. Use the media correctly and be friendly to them.

Weapon **61**

Join your People in Community Works

It is not enough to encourage and motivate the people to participate in constructing classrooms, teachers and health centre buildings etc. It is not even enough to contribute money and building materials. Get time to participate with them in doing community works. The Father of the Nation, Mwalimu Julius K. Nyerere, did exactly that between 1967 and 1977. You can also do the same.

If your Vehicle has Free seats, Offer a Lift

Apart from vehicles carrying leaders, which are prevented from doing so, or national leaders with special protocol and special defense, it is good, if your vehicle has unoccupied seats, to offer lifts, but, to people you know (so that you don't give lift to armed robberers), especially to sick people and pregnant women, waiting for transport to hospitals or clinics or those returning home from the same, disabled people and other people in need of transport. But, even so, do not allow excess people into your vehicle as this will be breaking the traffic law and you might end up paying penalties. Observe the law strictly.

If your vehicle is full, stop and tell them so. They will understand you well and you will have no blame. You will be blamed if you did not stop to talk to them. As I told you in Weapon 27, never drive past people while the windows of your vehicle are closed.

Do not Resolve a Dispute by Listening to one side

After becoming a leader, many people will come to you with different problems. Some will be accusing or complaining against fellow citizens or neighbours. Some will be complaining about your fellow leaders or officers in your office or public offices or offices of your fellow leaders.

Coming to you is normal. It also shows that they believe in your ability to resolves their conflicts and they love you.

Listen to him/her carefully, write down whatever he/she says, but, do not reach conclusion or believe in what has been narrated to you by one side. To get the truth, arrange for another day so that the accused can also attend. On that day, when both are present, let him/her repeat the same narration in the presence of the accused, so that the accused person can ask him or her questions and present his points of view on the same issue. This is exactly what magistrates and judges do in the courts of law. They don't judge by listening to one side. The accused person has also right to be heard.

If you stand by this principle, many people who have the habits of accusing others without concrete facts will shy away and will never come to you. Most of them are habitual architects of conspiracies and intrigues. As a weapon, I advise you that, in your life, you should never resolve a case or conflict between people by listening to one person. Doing so will reduce the number of people coming to you with accusations and will minimize conspiracies and intrigues and you will be respected for that. Neither will you be associated with these vices.

You should Not Engage Yourself in Gossip and Intrigues

"Gossip" is unfounded rumours and hearsay. Gossip is defined as a secret plan of something illicit or detrimental to someone else. In other words, it involves secret plans to do something illicit or detrimental to someone. Gossips are untrue words or false information spoken by a person about one or more persons for his/her own evil intentions. It is a behaviour of a person to propagate words or false information about another person with the aim of defaming him/her. Take an example of a place of work (like an institution etc) where one employee decides to tell the Chief Executive Officer (employer) bad things, which in reality not true, about his Head of Department so that he can be fired from the position, hoping that he would replace him as head of the said department.

On the other hand, intrigues are a behaviour of a person to say words or information which will result in agitation, cause dissension, make trouble or bring about misunderstandings between people.

You, as a leader, should refrain from engaging yourself from gossips and intrigues against other people. If you do so, your leadership will be in problems. Many people will hate and despise you. It is not good to be associated with these vices. Neither should you associate yourself with people who are habitual to gossips and intrigues. They are dangerous people to you and your leadership. They will make you hate people and you will also make them be hated by people. If this is so, who will you lead?

Weapon 65

You Should not use Narcotics and Cannabis, Don't manufacture them, Don't Grow their crops and Don't sell them

Narcotics are of many kinds. Some are plants grown by farmers. These include bhang and khat. Others, such as cocaine and heroin are manufactured from certain chemicals. These narcotics destroy the health of users, especially, the youth. They destroy their mental faculties and their bodies and consequently reduce a country's labour force. These narcotics are poisons that kill users slowly.

You, as a leader, should not use them, sell them, facilitate its business in the country, grow their crops nor manufacture (make) them. This is illicit business. You cannot participate in incapaciting and killing your people, especially the youths, the labour force of this country.

A person dealing in these narcotics should not be elected or appointed to lead people. If he is already a leader, he/she should not be allowed to continue leading.

Let it be known, that, any person engaged in this dirty business is a killer of the people, especially the youth, who are the labour force of this country.

You Should Be a True Nationalist

A Nationalist is a person who feels proud for and loves his country. This is his country. He loves it and is ready to defend it and its people and is ready to pay the highest price while defending it and its people. A nationalist is ready to use all his talents, energy, education and dedication to contribute to the development of his country. He is ready to contribute whatever he has to raise the welfare and standard of living of the people. However, note that not every citizen or a person born in this country is a true nationalist. We have heard of traitors, saboteurs, armed robberers, killers of innocent people, terrorists etc. These are not nationalists, although they are citizens of the country.

A leader must be a true nationalist and uses his intelligence, diligence and energy to build and defend his country and make highest contribution to the development of his country.

At all times, he/she is ready to defend it and its people. A true nationalist cannot hide his nationalism. You can see that in is his everyday life, his speeches and his contributions of ideas in open and indoor meetings.

A leader who is a nationalist is truthful and transparent. A nationalist leader believes and fights for the rights of children, women, disabled people and human rights. A nationalist leader is not discriminatory, not lazy, not a liar, not corrupt, not a robberer and not a swindler.

You should Neither be Arrogant nor Nuisance

Arrogance is a feeling that a person sees himself better or superior to others. He is self-lauding, he is conceit. On the other hand, a nuisance is a difficulty person, a person who causes problems or trouble and is annoying others. He enjoys annoying others and he is not cooperative with other people. A leader should neither be arrogant nor a nuisance. A leader should always see himself as a servant of the people who elected him to office or appointed by the authority to lead them. If he sees himself as a servant of the people, how can he see himself as a better or superior than the people who put him into office, who made him their leader? How can he tell the authority that appointed him that he is superior or better than the people he was given to lead? Or, how can he/she show his people that he is nuisance.

Arrogance and nuisance are not for any person, especially, a leader. At all times a leader sees himself/herself small to the people he leads, although the people see him as their superior. Let them see you that way and not you to see yourself that way. A leader should show humbleness, humility and self-abasement to the people he leads. If he/she does not do that people will not continue to support you as their leader, they will not elect you in the next election and if you are an appointed leader you will not be allowed to continue leading them or you will not be reappointed. If you are a religious leader, you might continue leading the folk (believers), but they no longer love you and they don't like you to continue leading them. If that is the case, your leadership is sour   and you will not enjoying it or be happy with it.

Do not make People's Complaints Secret

People's complaints should not be made secret. For this reason, if you receive or hear people's complaints of any kind, do not sit on them or make them secret. Make them public so that they may be addressed to quickly and openly by all people concerned or responsible.

If you make them secret, it will take a long time for the people responsible to take action or no action will ever be taken. That being the case, people's complaints will not be solved, mistreatments, injustices, oppressions, will prevail, implementation of their projects will stall, their rights will continue being suppressed etc.

Weapon **69**

You Should Not be a Thief, Armed robberer or a Corrupt Leader

The harmful effects of thievery of any kind, armed robbery and corruption etc to an individual, a group of people, society and a country are well known. People's properties are stolen, deaths of people increase, injustices and oppressions prevail, human rights are compromised, development stalls etc. A leader must not practice these vices or even be associated with them in anyway. Instead, openly and in public he must condemn them and dissociate himself with all persons suspected to do so and must take stern actions to uproot them from the society and assist law enforcers to take legal action on all people suspected of doing so. People should believe that you're serious and committed to see these vices eradicated from the society in your area of leadership and beyond.

If you do so, people will love you, because they will see you that you are unhappy with these law breakers. If, on the other hand, you don't, people might assume, righty or wrongly that you bless these people and their vices and you profit from them.

You should never be suspected to be associated with these law breakers and their vices. It is very dangerous to you and your leadership to do so.

You Should Not be Very Hot tempered and not Easily Angered

Temper is the state of talking with fume. Hot temper is not good for a leader. However, temper on the lower scale is necessary for a leader. For example, you cannot realize that people under you or leaders of lower levels have not implemented your orders, or resolutions passed by a meeting or orders from above and not be angry or keep silent. If you don't do so, you will be regarded as a simpleton and they will let you down. The temper that is not allowed for a leader is to be hot tempered or to be excessively tempered. If you be so, those responsible will dissociate themselves from you or they will go on strike.

On the other hand, every human being has some degree of anger. Any person who has no anger at all is not human. May be he/she is an angel! What is not allowed for a leader is to be easily angered. It is dangerous and disadvantageous to posses this behaviour. This is because, once you are a leader, there are many reasons to make you angry. Your role is to control your anger. Even if it happens that you are angry, people should not notice it. Don't show it to people. Control your anger. Laugh or smile in situations where you would show anger. If you are provoked by any person, laugh or smile instead of being angry at him/her.

That is leadership. A character of easily becoming angry is not good. You should not be a champion of getting angry easily. Do not forget the Kiswahili saying, *"Hasira hasara."* Meaning *"Anger is loss."* Anger can lead you to misbehaving, fighting and even to cause bodily harm to others or even to cause deaths.

If you do so eventually you will end up in police custody and in the court of law for your misdeeds. You may end up being fined, imprisoned or even hanged. If any of these happen to you, you might lose your leadership. Why then, should all these happen to you, when you can prevent them happening by controlling your anger.

Be Happy and Celebrate Achievements of your People

Achievements of your people are achievements of your leadership. When they celebrate them, join them and celebrate with them. The achievements can be of an individual, a family, a group, a SACCOS, Foundation, Sub-village, Village, Street, Ward, Division, an election constitueny, District Council, Town Council, Municipal Council and City.

To the extent possible, be happy and celebrate achievements of your people. Drum up, sing, eat and drink with them etc. In so doing, you will have cooperated with them in these events and your will have consolidated yourself with them. They will see you as being one of them.

Weapon **72**

Often Present a Performance Report of what you do to your Electors

If you are an elected leader, people who elected you gave you a job for a certain period, which can be a year, two or five; often it is a period of five years. You are expected every after a certain period, may be two or three months, to call a public meeting and tell them what you have done during that period and close to the end of the period you will give an annual performance report. Tell them your achievements and problems you encountered during implementation and efforts done to remove or minimize them.

Give them enough time to discuss the Report, to discuss you, to discuss the institution you lead or which you are associated with. They will certainly have complaints, comments, opinions, frustrations, advices, suggestions etc. All these will be intended to make you perform better during the coming period. Work on them and their analysises of the report.

Many leaders forget or ignore this weapon. They wait till the end of their period of leadership. Your electors will not understand you and they will not respect you because you don't respect them. If you are a counselor you should go to every sub-village or street to present your report. If you are a Member of Parliament do the same. If you are the President you are not exempted.

This weapon is meant for all leaders and of all categories, governmental, political, religious, NGOs etc.

Respect your electors by often presenting performance reports of the work they elected you for.

76

Weapon **73**

You should be a Thankful Person

There is a saying that goes, "If you cannot thank a human being you will not thank God." People say, "To say thank you for whatever good accorded to you is to ask for more."

Many elected leaders often forget or ignore this weapon. Soon after election, visit many places in the area of your leadership to thank people who elected you, and those who did not, for giving you an opportunity to lead and save them. All are your subjects and you have the moral duty to serve them without discrimination of any kind. Thank them earnestly and promise to serve them prudently, diligently, disciplinary and by observing the country's constitution, laws and by-laws guiding the institution you lead. Request for their assistance and cooperation in executing your duties. Also, seek God's guidance in your leadership.

For those leaders elected by a General Meeting, thank the delegates inside the conference hall, but soon, thereafter go to thank those members who elected and sent them to attend the meeting which elected you. This can be done in closed and/or open meetings.

You cannot put a monetary value to the word "thanks", but, its value is very huge, worthy of billions of shillings.

Weapon 74

Provide a monthly Income and Expenditure Report of the Institution you lead

Many conflicts we often hear in the governments of villages, cooperative societies, SACCOS, Nongovernmental organizations, Primary Schools, Secondary Schools, Institutes, Colleges, Universities, Offices of political parties of all levels, religious institutions etc arise because the leaders refuse or delay intentionally presenting to the people responsible Income and Expenditure Reports every month or every after a certain period.

This is a result of leaders and officer(s) in that particular institution not agreeing on how the money contributed by the people or granted to the institution was spent. Sometimes one side (the leader or the officer(s) is responsible for the misuse of the money or both, have collaborated in misusing it. Often times the money has been "stolen" or has been misused, and those responsible are afraid of being disciplined by the people who elected or appointed them or are afraid of being taken to courts of law.

If there were no discrepancies in the use of the money, reports would have been released in time. Not doing so, is to deny the people of their rights, is to delay implementation of the projects in question, is to invite complaints, strikes, disputes, doubts and damage to properties of schools, institutions concerned or of the leader.

As a leader, you must understand well damages which can result if these reports are not presented in time. Not doing so might affect your respect and good name, including associating you with thefts and cheating assumed to have been committed.

Therefore, if, in one way or the other you are or your are not involved in misusing the money contributed by the people or/granted to the institution, prepare and present Income and Expenditure Reports every month. The Reports must be correct and open, the annual one must be audited by a qualified Auditor. You should not hide anything in those Reports involving public money. In the reports, show date and numbers of Receipts, Invoices, Payment Vouchers, cheques, full names of payers and payees. All financial books and documents must be well written and preserved for inspection and verifications by internal and external auditors.

Weapon **75**

You should Not Fear to hold Meetings with People you Lead

We have heard of strikes in some of the secondary schools, institutes, colleges, religious denominations etc. We have head leaders of some villages, nongovernmental organizations, cooperative societies, SACCOS etc being accused by members of the organizations to the national leaders so that they can be told how their organization a fairing as there are no meetings held to discuss different issues.

We have heard of what happens when strikes occur in schools and higher learning institutions: there are damages to properties belonging to the institutions and teachers/ lecturers in resulting in all students or the ring leaders being sent back home, some of them discontinued from continuing with studies because they were the leaders of the strike etc.

If we investigate the main cause of the strike, it is because the heads of the institutions ignored, refused or delayed in holding meetings with the students and teachers so that they can explain to them how the institution is fairing, the financial affairs, progress, projects, challenges and problems. In these meetings the students and teachers will take the opportunity to ask the administration questions which will be answered; they will also give their opinions, comments and suggestions. If you do this routinely, you can be sure there will be no strikes!

Because these heads of institutions do not hold meetings with the students, they appear to have put up a wall or a curtain between them and the students. The latter would have raised their grievances, they would have raised several and different questions and the heads would have replied to their satisfaction and by doing so would avert strikes or unrest in the community.

By not getting explanations and clarification on different issues that concern them early and timely, students (sometimes under instigation of some of their teachers/ lectures) strike and destroy properties. This also happens to all other institutions mentioned earlier. To fear, neglect or to delay meeting people you lead is a big weakness in their ability to lead. Why should you fear? What are you trying to hide? Remember that your fear means death or loss to the people you lead. Do not fear. You are their leader.

Do not do the business that involve Black marketing

Black marketing is buying or selling goods to people in other countries contrary to the laws of the country, often hiding the goods so that they don't be seen by the government arms, that's the police and other authorities. It is a prohibited type of business. Black marketing involves crops and crop products, animals and animal products, industrial products etc. To do this type of business is to avoid paying government taxes and to contravene other regulations of the country. What each country requires of its citizens is to obey the country's laws and other statutory instruments in place. This type of business has other disadvantages, like endangering the lives of the operators (of the business), the vehicles and other transportation means used to ferry the goods might be destroyed or confiscated by the government. There are many other disadvantages.

Because of these disadvatages, a leader should not do such business. You should be a good example to your people in respecting the country's laws.

You should not Destroy Economic Infrastructures

Examples of infrastructures are roads, bus stations, railway rails, airports, ports etc. Destruction of these and other infrastructures include removing the rails, destroying the roads, airports, removing road signs etc. You should not participate in doing so as it may result, among other disadvantages, in causing accidents, shortening the life span of the same, stoping operations of factories and other industrial operations which use goods transported by the same, paralyzing transportation systems in the country etc.

So, protect them and educate your people on the importance of protecting economic and other infrastructures. You should be a good example to your people in protecting these lifelines of the economy of the country.

Weapon **78**

Participate in Conserving the Environment

Environment is the totality of all things surrounding creatures, including the air, land, water, the lives of insects, birds, planes and animals including human beings; buildings, economic infrastructures, machines and similar man-made objects, matter, gas, climate, temperatures, sound etc. The lives of human beings are greatly influenced and dependent on the environment. The development of a country is greatly influenced and dependent on its environment.

Destroying the environment is destroying life on earth. One of the effects of doing so is climate change. We now all see the negative effects being inflicted on mankind by climate change.

On the other hand, some of the major actions poluting and destroying the environment include:

- Destruction of the land, including soil erosions of all kinds.

- Destruction of forests and natural covers of the land.

- Destruction of the "homes" of wild creatures and biosystems.

- Destruction of the natural "homes" of waterborne creatures.

- Pollution of the air, water etc.

Doing the opposite of these actions such as planting trees, keeping manageable number of livestock, control of soil erosions. Doing so is protection or conserving the environment.

Because of these disadvantages, you should not pollute or destroy the environment. You, as a leader of people, should be role model in conserving the environment and encourage your people to do the same.

Weapon 79

You should not be Selfish

Selfishness is lacking consideration for others; concerned chiefly with one's own personal profit or pleasure. A selfish person does not want another person to own assets. He/she does not want others to be better than him or to be equal to him or to be as rich as he/she is. A selfish person is envious, jealous and aggressive. A selfish person always sees himself/herself as the only person who has the right to everything good or profitable.

On the other hand, nobody wants to be friend or be associated with a selfish person. He/she does not deserve that honour.

You, as a leader, should never be selfish. Give chance to all persons to use their intelligence, diligence and resources available in the country to become successful in their lives.

Weapon **80**

Do not use your Position of Leadership to Enrich yourself Speedly

To enrich one is not bad in itself. What is not allowed is to use your leadership to enrich yourself very speedily by all means, including using unlawful means, like doing black marketing business, involving yourself in armed robbery, soliciting corruption, selling illicit drugs, denying people their rights, doing injustice to your people etc.

Because of this, do not be selfish. If you are, stop it. If you have never been one, never think of being so.

Weapon **81**

Never hold many Leadership positions at the same Period

It is a human character to accumulate for oneself properties, assets, praise or credentials. But, if this character becomes excessive or too much, then it is not desirable. For instance, if you are a village chairman, a Counselor, a Member of Parliament etc at the same period, you will be labelled as greed for leadership positions and there are disadvantages. There is a saying "he who holds two pieces of something simultaneously, one of them will drop away without your knowledge or wish."

It is impossible to do justice to all these positions. After all you are a human being. Remember that even one position is a burden and some people fail to do justice to it. What about if they are two or more? My advice is that you should be satisfied with holding one leadership position at one period. However, you are permitted to change positions, that is at the expiry of the current leadership period, you can leave it and contest for another new position. Let other people hold available leadership positions. Instead of you occupying two or more positions, occupy one and let other two or more people occupy the other positions. In this case, at the same period, there will be two or more leaders, including yourself, instead of one in your area? It will be a team of leaders instead of one man's show! The people stand to gain more from the team working together rather than one person working alone.

In this case, you will be a role model of good leaders and people will love you and will help you make a success of your leadership.

Do Not Retain your Camp after Election

Normally, during a campaign period leading to Election Day, a campaigner for a position assembles a campain team composed of staunch supporters, close and committed friends. This is normal and permissible. It is obvious that if you want to win an election you must have a team composed of royal staunch supporters made up of people representing different sections of the electorate: the youth, women, farmers, workers, religious denominations, the disabled people, senior citizens, retired politicians, etc who will help win for you supporters and votes from those groups. Without doing so, how can you win the contested position? So, camps are necessary and welcome.

However, after winning or losing, the camp should be disbanded. The camp to remain intact is a mistake, because for a long time to come you will be dividing your people into two categories: the first one will be composed of people very close to you and the second one will be composed of the rest. This will be dangerous to the unity of your political party or your organization which sponsored you for the just ended election, your area of leadership or your country.

For this reason, a leader should not retain or keep intact your camp after the election is over.

Weapon **83**

Don't See Yourself Better than the People you lead or Your Fellow Leaders

The slogan that, "we need best leaders and not mere leaders" is not new to many people in this country. During election period, placards are put up in different places urging people to elect the best leaders and not mere leaders.

It is our hope that on the election day people will elect the best and capable leaders to lead them.

So, those elected to leadership should regard themselves as the best and capable leaders and not the opposite. What is prohibited in this weapon is to be boastful to people that you are the best leader or person compared to all the people you lead or fellow leaders you cooperate with to lead the people. This is a mistake of praising yourself, being conceited and you will be regarded as a leader without wisdom and prudence.

This weapon is mainly for both elected and appointed leaders, at all levels of leadership, in this country.

Let people see you as the best leader and not you to brand yourself so.

Weapon **84**

Commit yourself to Serve your Country and her People

This country will be developed and defended by her people under the guidance of their leaders. As their leader, you are expected to commit yourself wholly heartedly, with all your intelligence, energy, dedication and diligence to serve your country and her people. As a leader you have more opportunities to contribute to the development and defense of your country and her people than the ordinary people you lead. Commit yourself and encourage people to do the same, everyone to the extent he/she can manage and according to his/her ability.

These are many ways to do so, including, working hard, adding more hours working, increasing your efficiency at work and by being more disciplined at work and in your everyday life.

Weapon **85**

Realize that your Position is a Collateral and do not Use it or that of Another Person to your Advantage

Collateral is an asset or property a person gives to you to keep for a specific period and for a special reason. It is normally given as a security for something else. We are used to hearing of collateral for a loan, implying that should someone who obtained a loan from a financial institution fail to pay it back with interest, it (the institution) will sell the same to recover the amount of money owed.

For leadership, your position or title is collateral, meaning that if you do not perform to the satisfaction of the people who elected you or to the satisfaction of your appointing authority, you will lose it.

Your position is a collateral, and it means that it belongs to the people who elected you or the authority which appointed you, and has been given to you to keep for them or him/her for a specific period. That time is the period during which you will perform to their/his/her satisfaction. Not doing that, they/he/she will take it from you. So, your leadership position is not yours, it has been given to you to keep it for the said reason and period.

You have been given this position to use it to serve and lead well the people given to you to lead or the people who elected you. The position may be withdrawn anytime or rejected by the people who elected you if you don't perform to their satisfaction.

So, because your current leadership position is not your personal property, it is a collateral, do not use it or that of another person to your advantage except to the advantage of the people you lead and the whole country. Also, during the period you are holding the position, work hard, diligently, with all your wisdom, energy and prudence so that you don't lose it. The choice is yours.

Commit Yourself to Fight Poverty, Ignorance, Diseases and Oppression

Once you have been elected or appointed a leader, you have been given ample opportunity to serve your people in many different ways.

Your duty is to commit yourself to fight poverty, ignorance, diseases and oppressions of different types prevailing among your people. By your position, the opportunity is there for you to serve your people. Use it well and fully for the benefits of all the people. The letter will reward you in turn.

You can do so by representing well your people and speaking for them and on their behalf in the forums of which you are a member, such as the Councils and Parliament. By encouraging them to work hard, to value education, expecially, of thier children. By participating in the construction of dispensaries, health centres, schools and by the people refusing to be exploited, corrupted and oppressed in any way. You should educated your people to fight for their rights and demand them. The people should demand democrary in thier every day life. People should be educated on the resources available in thier vacinity and country for use in order to end poverty, ignorance and diseases. The end goal is their development.

So, commit yourself to work for the welfare of your people so that they can raise the standards of living.

Admit making Mistakes, Agree to be corrected and Apologize to the People for Mistakes you made

To make mistakes is human. We are told that only God does not make mistakes. Angels and all creatures, including human beings, do make mistakes. But, there are some people who do not admit that they make mistakes, although they do make them. Apart from "mistakes" taken to court for determination, where, if you admit easily the same you will have judged yourself. Other mistakes should not be included in this category.

The mistakes referred in this weapon are those related to your daily leadership, social mistakes, political mistakes, matrimonial mistakes, family mistakes etc. Failing to admit these types of mistakes is mere ignorance, is to show your arrogance and is to deny respect for your people and fellow leaders. A courageous leader is when he/she unfortunately makes a mistake, will weigh it, then he/she will look for a way, language or a respectable way of admitting it to those he/she thinks he/she has offended. After this admission, he/she will look for an opportunity and choose appropriate words or language, at the right time or occasion, to apologise to the people he/she believes he/she offended.

On the other hand, for the same logic, a good leader is that one who publicly admits or seeks to be corrected by the people he leads without feeling offended. When corrected, you should not feel offended, because you have been made strong and you will feel relieved and happy that the heavy burden has been taken away from your shoulders. If you refuse to be corrected, you will remain with your ignorance and will remain a weak leader.

Those of you who are in marriage, remember the day when you apologized to your spouse and his/her anger ended immediately, and both of you became instantly happy, peace restored and good and happy life continued prevailing in your family. This is the power and advantages of seeking reconciliation by happily and willingly tendering your apology to the offended side.

On the other hand, a "lower" leader and the highest leader, like the President of a nation, can make a mistake or mistakes. A mistake does not choose a leadership position or age. Both young and old persons do make mistakes. Any leader can offend people below or above him. But, all deserve and it is their right to demand their leader to admit the mistake, agree to be corrected and to apologize to them.

A leader who apologises after admitting making mistakes and seeks to be corrected, should be sure he will be pardoned by the people he apologized to. Any person who will not pardon him will have his own reasons, but, he should remember that any person who refuses to pardon people who sincerely apologized, will not be pardoned by others.

In general, people like to be lead by a person who has the heart and courage of admitting making mistakes and seeking to be pardoned by the people he believes he offended. Besides, people like to be lead by a leader who admits willingly, happily and with a white heart to be corrected when he makes mistakes.

You should not deny yourself this weapon. Be with it wherever you will be in your life.

Weapon 88

You must be Courageous

Courage is the ability of a person to face a serious situation without fear. A courageous person is brave, hero and is able to take up serious and challenging issues and manage them well. A leader should be courageous. There are times, periods or situations which demand you to be courageous and your people expect you to show that you are really brave and a hero, otherwise, you will be judged as a cowardice and timid, and that you are not able to defend your people when challenges happen.

During difficult times, you should come out and be seen that you are available and strong to handle the situation. You should neither hide yourself nor your face. If you do so, where do you want the people you lead to go? Should they appear orphans?

You must be seen that you are ready to die or to be affected by your appearance, (instead of hiding yourself). Do not allow your people to be negatively affected when you are able to reduce the impact of the effects or to prevent the effects from happening to them.

There is no leadership that is easy. Times are not the same. There are times when there is turmoil. There are also hard or difficulty times, full of danger, turmoil, there are times when the leaders and those lead become hostile to each other, there are times when people are hungry, killings and armed robbery are on the increase in town and rural areas, people do not come up to contribute to the construction of their schools, dispensaries and students in schools are on strikes etc. In such times, you must prove to them that you are really courageous by coming out and issue a statement or make an announcement aimed at restoring the situation to normality. In such situations, you are not expected to show a happy face or laugh. You must show that you have been annoyed and angered. You must be on the side of the majority. You must defend the country's constitution, laws and by-laws. You must shout at people breaking the constitution, laws and by-laws. You must prove that you are in control or you are contributing to the normalisation of the situation.

Develop Tomorrow's Leaders

To-day's leaders, you included, are to pass (they will not be there tomorrow). They are not permanent in this world. Any leader can leave leadership anytime because of sickness, death, resignation, revoking an appointment, ending of the leadership period, not being re-elected, not being re-appointed, and being dismissed from leadership because you no longer have the required qualifications to lead.

Because of this, a good leader is that one who develops or contributes to development of future leaders, leaders of tomorrow. Don't develop one or two. Develop many people for each category of leadership.

The main reason is to have a bank of many qualified people for leading people tomorrow. Normally, people being developed are the youth, aged 20-45 years. The younger the better. But, they must be well educated, versed in many issues and aspects of leadership. They must have been given a chance to attend different courses in leadership of people, economic development, defense, entrepreneurships, politics of the country, the economy etc. If he did not complete (still better if he passed) Form IV or its equivalent, it will be difficult for him/her to lead people. A diploma or at least the first degree is preferable these days.

A leader who does not develop tomorrow's leaders is useless, is selfish, is stingy, is a coward and not brave. He is not fit to be a leader of this country.

Good leaders are developed for a purpose. Your country needs to be lead by people who have been developed well and qualified for leadership, as said above in all aspects of development, that's in politics, social, cultural scientific and socially, economic development, in the civil and public services; in science, technology, arts etc, it is leadership in totality. Participate in this important duty. You cannot afford not to do so.

Weapon **90**

You Should Not be a "Killer" of fellow Leaders

There are leaders who do not want to see fellow leaders excel in their leadership. They are happy if they perform poorly or they fail. They are happy if they participated in their failures!

They want themselves to continue shining and excelling others. This is their character, which is dangerous. In order to succeed in their evil intentions, they are ready do anything possible to spoil the leadership of fellow leaders. They will throw mud to them, they will plot bad things on them, they will accuse them of this or that, they will turn moulds of mistakes to look like mountains (of mistakes) etc.

Their evil target is to see that they are disqualified from leadership, they are removed from leadership or not re-elected, not re-appointed etc. If any of these happens, they will have achieved their evil intentions.

Do not be a leader of this type. Don't "kill" fellow leaders of any kind and level. You are expected to develop them, help them, correct them when they are not performing well to the expectations of the people who elected them or the authority which appointed them, so that they become better leaders than you.

A good leader is that one who is happy when other leaders perform well in leadership. For this reason, you will be proud to have contributed to their success and they will be happy of your contribution to their success and of what they are.

You Should Not be Doubted of Anything

The life of a leader is not confidential. Neither, is it expected to be confidential. A leader is seen even in darkness. You will be cheating yourself if you think that you are not seen by a person or persons just because it is darkness. You're seen. Because of this, do whatever you do openly, because even if you hide them, they will be seen. People you lead are curious to know your matrimonial life, your relationship with your children, parents, sisters, brothers, clan members, friends, neighbours, whether you are a believer in God or not, if you go to the place of worship as required by your religion, if you are hard working or lazy, your hobbies etc.

The people want to know you well in all these aspects and more, because the actions of a leader are contiguous. For this reason, they love to be lead by a good person and a person who fears God.

So, you should not try to hide who you are. Why should you hide your character and actions? If you do so, they will come out with their own conclusions about who you are, which, in some cases, might not be correct.

They might suspect you of what you are not, and they may not be always correct. If this is the case, why should you give them the opportunity to misunderstand or misjudge you?

For this reason, you should not be doubted of anything, including your citizenship, nationality, your nationalism, honesty, integrity, character, your personal and public life, behaviour etc. A leader should not be doubted of anything.

Weapon 92

You Should be a Faithful Parent Who can be Relied Upon

A leader is a co-parent (a father or mother) and a defender of your people, especial their children. You are the co-parent of all the children in the area of your leadership. However, we are aware that sometimes a parent can be good or bad to his/ her children. You are expected to be judged by your actions, daily life and statements (announcements) that you are a good parent and that you can be relied upon.

If you are known to be an adulterer or fornicator, running after people's wives, school girls/boys, young, middle and aged, fellow parents will fear to associate with you and will not trust you with their wives and especially their children. Besides, children will be afraid of you so that you do not infect their parents with sexually transmitted diseases, including HIV/AIDS.

If you are a thief, fellow parents will cast doubt on you that you will steal their school fees and other contributions. If you are lazy on working on the expansion of the educational facilities, like construction of classrooms and teacher's houses so that the quality of education provided to their children can be better, your fellow parents will see you as having no good intention of seeing their children receiving quality education.

A leader should be seen by parents, their children and the general public as reliable and faithful. Your reliability and faithfulness should be seen in your behaviour, character, your daily life and actions. The latter and whatever comes out of your mouth will show who you are.

Give heed to the Common people in the Society

In our society, be it a sub- village, village, a street, ward, division, district, region (province) or a country, the people can be placed into three main groups: the first one is the **common people,** in Kiswahili known as *Wanyonge*. These people are poor, some of them very poor, some of them leaving in extreme poverty, weak economically and wealthywise. They have a low standard of living and low social status. They live in poor housing, some have none. They regard themselves as neglected by the rulers, a belief that is contentious. They are the proletariat of the society. These people are the majority in the country and have the deciding power during political elections. They decide which political party should win elections and which candidates will win. For this reason, every political party and all contesting candidates promise these people that they will uplift their standard of living once elected, by paying more attention to them through channeling a big percentage of the resources and budget to them directly and indirectly.

The second group is composed of people with moderate richness. Their standard of living is much better than that of the first group. The third group is made of few people, but, very rich. Their standard of living is very high. They have all the basic necessities in plenty and in excess.

Because of the importance of the common people, especially during elections and because of their big numbers, a leader with wisdom and prudence should recognize this group, their importance in economic and social development and should show them by actions and pronouncements that he cares and respects them.

If you don't do so, they will revenge at an appropriate time. Heed them by encouraging them to work hard, diligently and with discipline. Care for them by making sure that their children go to school and be able to proceed to higher learning institutions, that's, colleges, institutes and universities. Care for them by looking for them assistances from within and outside the country, grants, soft loans, establishing projects that will stimulate their development, such as roads, railways lines, construction of schools and colleges, markets for their products, small industries, provision of improved seeds, improved breeds of poultry, animals etc. Encourage adult education so that those who are illiterate can learn how to read and write so that they move away from darkness to light. Educate them to stop drunkenness, especially drinking drinks that affect their health. Always remember that educating the children of poor people is the biggest contribution by you and the government to their development. This is what is being done in our country by constructing at least one primary school in each village, one secondary school in every ward, a High school (Forms V & VI) in every division, technical colleges in each district etc. With all these establishments and their literacy, there is every hope that the common people are on their way to the second group level, provided every able person works hard and has a determination to move out of this group.

If you, as a leader, be seen to be with this group in all the above and you will have given heed to them and they will always be with you, shoulder to shoulder.

Weapon **94**

Show Mercy on People Who get Disasters

Disaster is an event resulting in great loss of wealth, assets like buildings, crops, livestock, body and or life, which include extremely bad accidents, or natural calamity such as floods, earthquake or fire. Disasters cause financial and other losses, deaths, disabled people and people affected psychologically.

When a disaster strikes, you should immediately or soonest come out, be seen, and provide any assistance you can afford, inform the government at all levels so that it comes to their rescue. Be close to them, talk to them, sympathise with them, show sorrow with them, stay for longer periods with them during day and night times.

If it happens that you cannot personally be with them at the material time, send your representative (s), including your wife/ husband, mature son or daughter to represent you. They must introduce themselves that you sent them to represent you and deliver your message of sympathy and deliver whatever material assistance you can afford. Then, as early as possible, when you return, go straight to the site of disaster and meet the people affected. Console them. Talk to them and explain to them why you have come to visit them late.

If you do that, you will have shown them that you care and you have mercy on them. On the other hand, if you don't do that, they will see you as a leader who does not care about what inflicts them and that you are not one of them. They might wish you also to be struck by a disaster!

Weapon **95**

Invite Neighbours and Other People to be Friends of your People

The people you lead do not live a solitary life. For this reason, they want to live in peace with neighbours. They like to be associated and cooperate with other people far from them. This is why even at national level, a President travels to other countries (neighbouring and those far away) to establish friendship and good relationship with his country. Presidents of other countries also visit his country for the same reason. When they do so, they establish friendship of country to country and people to people.

Once we are friends, we can do and achieve a lot together. We can help each other in the fields of business, tourism, economic development, receiving assistance, grants, educate their children, have peace etc.

You should do the same at your level. By so doing you will have helped your people have peace, security, friendship with neighbours and people far away, receive assistance and grants for developments of all kinds etc. Encourage development, peace, security and happiness for your people. So, it is advisable to you to invite neighbours and other people to be friends of your people, for friendship pays.

Do not Cling to Leadership for a Long Period

Leadership is sweet. It is associated with high respect in society, prestige, social status, and allowances and amenities. Once you are made a leader, you have been given an opportunity to be seen by people, to be known, to be praised, to sit on the high table and on a good chair, to be seen with national leaders: the Ministers, Prime Minister, Vice President and President. The longer you stay in leadership, the more you become addicted to these amenities and privileges.

But, it so happens that, if, you stay in one leadership position for too long, your importance and prominence decreases very much. To the people you leader, you have nothing new. You have no new ideas. You have become so used to them and they are tired of you. They reach a stage when they think and believe that you see yourself that there is no one else who can replace you, a belief that is not correct. Often, it becomes hard for you to realize that people are tired of you and that they want a change of leadership.

On the other hand, the longer you stay in leadership, the more you fear leaving it, imagining if you leave leadership what type of person you will be? How will the people receive you? Will those people you annoyed or deprived of their rights pardon you or not? What will happen to your friends, relatives and family members? These are disturbing questions which have no easy answers.

On the other hand, during the period you have been clinging to your position, these are people in your area who, for a long time, have been preparing to take up your position and they have the required qualifications to lead, but, by using your position, strategies, intrigues, experience, even corrupt means, you prevented them from removing you. You do not want to leave voluntarily.

What they will do in order to remove you is to resolve to do so with whatever cost! They will remove you. Strategies they plan to use include looking for your weaknesses, your mistakes, to soil you, to fabricate scandals, to spoil your business, to expose your private life, your matrimonial affairs, your family life, to accuse you of anything, even on fabricated cases, to insult you in public, to take you to police and courts even if they are sure they will not win the cases etc.

They will do anything to you, right or wrong, their sole aim being to disqualify you from winning next election or to be removed from your appointed position, before the current period of your leadership ends.

If this is the pressure on you, for certain you will leave leadership in disgrace and all the good things you did for your people will be forgotten by the same people. You are solely responsible for this situation.

My advice is that you should not cling to leadership for a long period. Are one, two or three periods not enough for you? Answer this question for yourself.

Keep Secrets and Do not Spread Rumours

Once you are a leader, you have been given a chance to know a lot of information. This is a result of the many indoor and open meetings you attend, many documents that are sent to you or which you are given to you as a leader and the opportunity you have to talk to leaders including those above you.

Among the informations that you will receive or hear (by virtue of your being a leader), many are classified   as open and others as Confidential, Secret and Top Secret. Some information can only be made public by national leaders such as the Prime Minister, Vice President or the President at the right time and others will never be made public for many reasons, including security and safety of the country.

There are others which are recommendations of lower meetings for higher ones to make decisions. If you make known the recommendations of low meetings and if it happens that they are revised or rejected by higher meetings, you will have caused riots among your people and you will certainly pay the price.

It is a big mistake for a leader to reveal or make public information which is Confidential, Secret, Top Secret or sensitive, without getting permission from the authority. If you do so, you can cause loss, turmoil, disaster or even deaths. Also, if you are known to have done so, legal and disciplinary action may be taken against you.

Also, as a leader, you are prohibited from spreading rumours. The latter are information which has no proven truth or legality. It is hearsay. These are words or information which is unbelievable. Yet, some silly people spread the same for their evil intentions.

It should be a taboo for you to spread rumours, because they are dangerous to people and the area you lead and for the safety of your area and country. Either, it is bad behavior and character to do so. This may also lead to you being despised and disregarded by the people you lead and fellow leaders. This will disqualify you from continuing to lead people.

Weapon **98**

Acknowledge that your Children are Part of your Leadership

Your children are the result of your marriage. You and your wife/husband brought them into this would and both of you have the duty to bring them up. You, your spouse and children make up a family and your major role, as parents, is to bring up well these children. Before you become a leader, you performed this duty well with your spouse. But, after becoming a leader your time become scarce and most of the responsibilities of bringing up the children is left to one spouse. The effects of children being brought up by a single parent (while the other is alive) are many and could be serious. It is not good to enumerate them, but, we all know some of them, if not all.

But, these children continue to be yours both and they are referred to as the children of the leader. For them to be referred so may have advantages, but, also, disadvantages. Think about the time when your leadership was in turmoil, when you were unjustly accused, when you were despised, failed re-election or your appointment was revoked etc, your children had to bear all these circumstances, although they could also be affected psychologically. Also, think of the opportunity they get by contributing to your happiness when you get elected, re-elected or appointment or re-appointment.

Who would question that your children are not part of your leadership? They are.

Acknowledge your Spouse as being Part of your Leadership

Many people, not all, get leadership after marriage. That means that, in most cases *marriage* comes before leadership. The state of married life changes when a spouse becomes a leader. This concerns both spouses. It may be positively or negatively, or both.

Before becoming a leader, the spouses had more time together, helping each other or cooperating in executing certain tasks, fulfilling the marriage obligations to their satisfaction and to their wish, cooperating in bringing up their children, helping each other in case of sickness of one of the spouses, their children, to receive guests and attend together prayers for the morning, midday, evening, night and at meals.

After getting leadership, things do change. The first change is that for majority of days of the year, the leader is not at home, and even if he returns home, it will be late night. Most of the days he is on journeys attending meetings, seminars, workshops, conferences, parliament or meeting leaders above him rankwise for consultations or briefing them on some issues concerning his/her area he/she represent. For a certain type of leadership, you might find out that out of 366 days in the year, for 200 days he is out of his home. The spouse is left alone taking care of the children, properties, and family business. On the other hand, the leader also misses his wife/husband and children.

As result, both spouses fail to fulfill their marriage obligations. This becomes an opportunity for the satan to penetrate their marriage and spoil the latter. Also, the children miss his/her love and contribution to their upbringing. Instead, they find themselves being raised by a single parent. At night, these two people, separated by distance, sleep as if they are not in marriage, enduring cold as usual! This state of affairs can cause complaints, some sensitive and others bad, within the marriage.

Also, it is not a secret that a spouse might mess- up the leadership of the other spouse by revealing family matters, matrimonial issues, by making disturbances, by causing misunderstandings in the family, by doing actions which will embarrass the leader, like beginning to do adultery or fornication, to fight persons of the opposite sex, just because you suspect them of running with your spouse, to abuse people, neighbours, to disrespect you, and to say bad things in public regarding your leadership.

Fortunately, many couples (in marriage) do not do that. They understand each other and they bear each other. That is why many leaders have their marriages intact, happy and in love.

But, to be a wife or husband of a leader requires you to have a strong heart, to preserve and to plug in your ears from what some people say about your spouse, including gossip-markers. If you do not plug in your ears, your marriage will be unstable and even may break down, ending in divorce.

Leadership has also its disgusts to your spouse, especially during campaign periods, when a leader is at loggerheads with the media, turmoil periods, when the people are fed up with you, the period of discussing the character of the leader, when the leader has been suspended from leadership or dismissed or failed to be re-elected or re-appointed. To bear all these, the spouse needs to have a strong heart.

But, even when you are happy, the drum dancers need to be two or more on stage to make the occasion memorable. The spouse takes position number one in making you happy of your success. Without her/him you will not enjoy your happiness to the peak.

All is work. To the couples in marriage of which one of them is a leader, who has made their marriage last happily during the whole leadership period, deserve to be congratulated. When a marriage starts shaking, even your leadership starts shaking. If it breaks up, the results are bad to your leadership and your the future of your children.

For this reason, if you see a person who has made a success of a leadership of any kind, be it in politics, government, non-government, companies etc, you should realize that your spouse has contributed much to it. For certain, your spouse has been part of your leadership and has contributed greatly to the success you have achieved in your leadership. He/she has scarified a lot. At times, she has been tortured, been backbitten, has endured, has plugged in her ears etc. There is no doubt he/she has contributed to your success.

When you reach the end of your leadership, congratulate yourself and your spouse and thank the Almighty God for his assistance and guidance and for enabling both of you to do what you did. To reach here, has not been easy task. Both of you deserve credit.

You must not be Coward and Must have a Strong Heart

When a person is elected or appointed a leader, his/her friends, family members and other people, with good intentions for him, send him/her messages on his/his mobile handset, letters, cards, phone him/her or visit him/her at home or in office to congratulate him/ her. However, there are others who *congratulate* him/her and also *sympathise* with her/him. Those who add the "sympathy" word have a good reason and message for him/ her, which is that, although he/she will hence start sitting on the front chair and high table, to be known and be written about a lot by the media, but, you must hence known that you have been given across to carry, which is neither small nor one, but, they are big and many crosses.

By common sense, many people think that leaders (not only political leaders but, also those in government, religions, non-government, institutions, family leaders etc.) are very happy people. They are wrong. It is the opposite, although there are certain days a leader enjoys his leadership, but on other days, it is carrying heavy crosses on behalf of the people he/she leads, or because of actions and pronouncements of the people he leads or his own. Once you are a leader, you cannot avoid being tired, being abused, being blamed, being backbitten, being accused of this or that etc.

Even leaders under your leadership when they make mistakes, it is you who will be blamed. For the President or Prime Minister, there is another worry or fear, that of being toppled by the army, of being killed by rebels etc.

The common outcome of this situation is that many leaders are always sick of diseases caused by their lives of worries, often being tired etc. These diseases include blood pressure, diabetes, heart diseases, mental and body tiredness and psychological diseases. Because of this, many leaders (not all) live on swallowing different kinds of tablets daily, so as to sustain life. Otherwise, they die before their age. If you want to prove this, inquire from the spouses of leaders or close people to the leaders.

However, despite many people knowing these negative effects of leadership, at election times, many people come out to contest vacant positions or seek to be appointed to leadership of different categories, be it in politics, government, non- government, companies, institutions, departments, sections etc. They don't fear death! They do not fear poor health. But, in order to continue being a leader **"you, must not be a coward and must have a strong heart."**

CURRICULUM VITAE OF THE AUTHOR

1. Full Name	Pius Bakengera Ngeze
2. Date of birth	21 October, 1943
3. Sex	Male
4. Place of birth	
- *Village*	Nyakivomo (now called Muganza)
- *Ward*	Muganza
- *Division*	Rulenge
- *District*	Ngara
- *Country of domicile*	Tanzania
5. Religion	Roman Catholic
- *Date of baptism*	24/12/1943
- *Date of 1st communion*	8/12/1957
- *Date of confirmation*	5/7/1958
6. Citizenship	Tanzanian
7. Marital status	Married with five children
8. Postal address	P.O.Box 1222, Bukoba, Tanzania

9. Telephone contact	0784 690277, 0768 023019
10. Email	ngezep@yahoo.co.uk
11. Residential address	TEPU House, Plot No.45 Block MDA Uganda Road, Municipal of Bukoba, Tanzania.
12. Education	
- *Primary school*	Muganza Primary School, Std I-IV 1954-1957.
- *Secondary School*	Ihungo Sec. School (Forms I-IV), 1962-1966.
- *University*	Makerere University College (of the University of East Africa) 1967-1970.
13. Academic Awards	- B. Agric.Sc.(Hons) of the University of East Africa, 1970
	- Certificate in Project Planning and Implementation of the University of Bradford, England
	- Diploma in Socialist Agriculture
	- Various certificates in several fields
14. National Service (Jeshi la Kujenga Taifa)	1970 -1973
15. Government Service	- Planning Officer (Agriculture) at Headquarters of the Ministry of Agriculture, 1970 -1972. - District Planning Officer, 1972- 1975.

	- Assistant Commissioner of Planning and Control, Office of the Prime Minister and Second Vice President, 1975-1977.
16. Languages Spoke	- Kishubi (mother tongue) - Kiswahili - English
17. Politics	- Joined TANU in 1970 - Joined CCM in 1977
18. Political Leadership	(a) TANU Branch Chairman, Office of the District Commissioner, Iringa, 1974-1975. (b) Member of the Executive Committee of TANU Branch, Prime Minister's office, 1975-1977. (c) Member of the National Executive Committee of TANU, 1977-1997 and 2002-2007. (d) Regional CCM Chairman (for Kagera Region), 1977-1997 and 2002-2007. (e) Member of Parliament for Ngara Constituency 1995 -2000.
19. Patronship	(a) Tanzania – Danish Red Cross AIDS Project (1986-1990). (b) Rulenge Development Association (RUDEA), 1995-2000.

	(c) Kagera Orphans Trust Fund (KOTF), 1993.
	(d) Rulenge Homestead Executive Committee (RHEC), 1999-2003.
20. Founder and Chairman	(a) Kagera Writers and Publishers Cooperative Society Limited (1987-1996).
	(b) Kagera Community Based Organisation for the Welfare of the Child (KACOBAC), 1991-1996.
	(c) Tanzania Agricultural and Modernization Association (TAMA), 2006 – 2016.
21. Member of the Board of Directors (Directorship) of:	(a) Iringa District Development Cooperation, 1972-1975.
	(b) Tanzania Livestock Development Authority, 1975-1977.
	(c) Tanzania Tea Authority, 1954-1987.
	(d) Kagera Sugar Company Ltd, 1990-1995.
	(e) Shirika la Uchumi na Kilimo la Kagera (SUKIKA), 1993.
	(f) State Travel Services Ltd, 1993-1994.
	(g) Tanzania Cigarette Co., 1993-1994.
	(h) Tanzania Standard Newspapers Ltd, 1993-1996.

	(i) Cooperative and Rural Development Bank (CRDB), 1993-1996.
	(j) Advisory Board, Bukoka Branch, 2001-2002.
	(k) Tanzania Posts Corporation, 1997-2005.
	(l) Tanzania Railways Corporation, 2005-2007.
	(m) Tanzania Coffee Board, 2008-2011.
	(n) Bukoba Regional Referral Hospital, 2017- present
22. Chairmanship of the Board of Directors of:	(a) Shirika la Uchumi na Kilimo la Kagera (SUKIKA), 1993.
	(b) State Travel Services Ltd, 1993-1994.
	(c) Cooperative and Rural Development Bank, 1993-1996.
	(d) CRDB Bank Advisory Board, Bukoba Branch, 2001-2002.
	(e) Tanzania Coffee Board, 2008-2011.
	(f) Bukoba Regional Referral Hospital, 2017- present.
23. Business	(a) Chairman and Managing Director of New Upendo Lodge Ltd (1996-present).

	(b) Chairman and Managing Director of Tanzania Educational Publishers Ltd, 1992-present. (c) Chairman and Managing Director of Kabanga Garden Hotels Ltd, 2010 - present.
24. Countries visited	Burundi, Kenya, Uganda, Rwanda, China, North Korea, South Korea, Japan, England, German, Swiss, Austria, India, France, Vietnam, etc.
25. The AWARD (TUZO) of The Sokoine University of Agriculture for "Distinguished Contribution in Advancement of Agriculture in Tanzania"	Conferred on me by the Chancellor during the 28th Graduation, on November 23, 2013. It was in recognition of my Distinguished Contribution to the Development of Agriculture in Tanzania for authoring 55 books on agriculture.
26. Certificate of Recognition by Baraza la Kiswahili la Taifa (BAKITA)	Was presented to me in 2005 in recognition of my writing many educational books in Kiswahili.
27. Articles published	Several in Kiswahili and English Newspapers in the country.
28. Papers for Seminars, Workshops and Conferences.	Several.
29. Author of published books	Has written and published over 72 titles in the field of Agriculture, Health, Environment, and Politics (see Appendix).

30. Hobbies	- Jogging
	- Reading books and newspapers.
	- Discussions on current affairs in the country and beyond.
31. Political leadership retirement	(a) Retired from political leadership on 7th September, 2007.
	(b) Now self- employed (see No.23 above).

A LIST OF BOOKS WRITTEN BY THE AUTHOR

(1970 – 2018)

No.	Titles of the books	Year first published	ISBN
1.	Ushirika Tanzania (*Co-operatives in Tanzania*)	1975	978-9987-07-037-4
2.	Misingi ya Kilimo Bora (*Principles of Modern Agriculture*)	1976	978-9987-07-0183
3.	Juhudi na Maarifa katika Kilimo (*Diligence and Technology in Agriculture*)	1980	978-9987-671-80-9
4.	Visumbufu vya Mazao Shambani (*Enemies of field Crops*)	1980	978-9987-426-36-2
5.	Mboji (*Organic Manures*)	1980	-
6.	Kanuni za Ukulima wa Kisasa (*Principles of Modern Farming*)	1981	978-9987-671-13-7
7.	Maswali na Majibu Kuhusu Kilimo cha Kisasa (*Questions and Answers on Modern Agriculture*)	1987	978-9987-671-55-7
8.	Mbolea ya Takataka (*Compost Manures*)	1981	-
9	Sayansi ya Udongo (*Elementary Soil Science*)	1983	978-9987-426-30-0
10.	Mkulima Stadi (*Modern Farmer*)	1985	-
11.	Agizo la Chato (*The Chato Declaration*)	1986	-
12	Maswali na Majibu Katika Kilimo (*Questions and Answers on Modern Agriculture*)	1987	978-9987-671-55-7

13.	HESAWA Mkoani Kagera *(Health, Sanitation and Water in Kagera Region)*	1991	9976-982-13-5
14.	Migomba: Uanzishaji na Utunzaji wa Shamba *(Bananas: Establishment and Maintenance of a Plantation)*	1991	978-9987-671-91-5
15.	Utengenezaji na Matumizi ya **Mboleavunde** katika Kilimo*(How to Make and Use Composite Manure in Farming)*	1992	978-9976-982-17-6
16.	Kutengeneza na Kutumia **Mboji** katika Kilimo *(How to Make and Use Organic Manure in Farming)*	1993	978-9987-671-81-6
17.	Mbolea za Viwandani *(Artificial Fertilizers)*	1993	978-9987-426-33-1
18.	Jifunze Kustawisha **Maharage ya Soya** *(Learn to How to Grow SOYA Beans)*	1993	978-9987-426-28-7
19.	Jifunze Kustawisha **Mboga** *(Learn How to Grow Vegetables)*	1993	978-9987-426-31-7
20	Jifunze Kustawisha **Viazi Vikuu** *(Learn How to Grow Yarms)*	1993	978-9987-426-35-5
21.	Banana and their Management	1994	978-9987-671-75-5
22.	Learn How to Grow Sweet Potatoes	2000	9966-917-11-X
23.	Learn How to Grow Soya Beans	2003	9966-917-12-8
24.	How to Keep Farm Account	2003	9966-917-32-2
25	Misitu na Hifadhi ya Mazingira *(Forests and Conservation of the Environment)*	2003	978-9987-671-02-1
26.	Watoto na Mazingira *(Children and Environment)*	2003	978-9987-671-26-8

27.	Mwongozo wa Uhasibu wa Shamba (*A Guide to Farm Accounting*)	2003	978-9987-671-01-4
28.	Kilimo Bora cha **Mahindi** (*How to Grow Maize*)	2003	978-9987-671-56-4
29.	Kilimo Bora cha **Maharage** (*How to Grow Beans*)	2003	978-9987-671-41-0
30.	Sayansi ya Mimea ya Mazao (*The Science of Crop Plants*)	2003	978-9987-671-38-0
31.	Nguzo za Kilimo (*Pillars of Agriculture*)	2004	978-9987-07-007-1
32.	Kilimo Bora cha **Muhogo** (*How to Grow Cassava*)	2004	978-9987-671-51-9
33.	Ustawishaji Bora wa **Chai** (*How to Grow Tea*)	2004	9987-671-95-0
34.	Ustawishaji wa **Mtama** (*How to Grow Sorghum*)	2004	978-9987-671-97-7
35	Ufugaji wa Samaki Vijijini (*Fish Farming in Villages*)	2004	978-9987-671-54-0
36.	Ufugaji wa Nyuki Vijijini (*Bee Keeping in Villages*)	2004	978-9987-671-52-7
37.	Jifunze Kustawisha **Viazi Vitamu** (*Learn How to Grow Sweet Potatoes*)	2007	978-9987-426-34-8
38.	Kilimo bora cha **Alizeti** (*How to Grow Sunflower*)	2007	978-9987-426-16-4
39.	Mwongozo Ufugaji Bora wa **Mbuzi** (*A Guide to Modern Goat Husbandry*)	2007	978-9987-671-53-3
40.	Kutoka **Uchungaji** Kwenda **Ufugaji** (*From Herding to Zero Grazing*)	2007	978-9987-426-17-4

41.	Uanzishaji, Ufufuaji na Utunzaji wa Shamba la Kahawa *(Establishment, Rehabilitation and Management of a Coffee Farm)*	2007	9987-426-18-2
42.	Ufugaji Bora wa **Kuku** *(Poultry Husbandry)*	2008	978-9987-07-016-9
43.	Silaha 100 za Kiongozi *(100 Weapons of a Leader Leadership)*	2008	978-9987-07-005-3
44.	Mwanzo na Mwisho wa Uongozi wa Kisiasa *(The Beginning and End of Political Leadership)*	2008	978-9987-07-010-7
45.	Ushuhuda wa Muujiza wa Mei 11, 2007 *(Witness of a Micracle on May 11, 2007)*	2008	978-9987-07-001-5
46.	Wanyonge Wasinyongwe *(The Weak Should Not Be Hanged)*	2008	978-9987-07-011-4
47	Jifunze Kustawisha **Viazi Mviringo** *(Learn How to Grow Round Potatoes)*	2009	978-9987-671-87-8
48.	Ufugaji Bora wa **Sungura** *(Rabbit Husbandry)*	2009	978-9987-07-017-6
49.	Ufugaji Bora wa **Nguruwe** *(Pig Husbandry)*	2009	978-9987-07-021-3
50.	Kanuni za Ufugaji Bora *(Principles of Modern Animal Husbandry)*	2009	978-9987-07-034-3
51	Mapinduzi ya Kilimo kwa Kutumia Zana Bora za Kilimo *(Green Revolution Through the Use of Agricultural Implements)*	2010	978-9987-07-042-8

52	Kilimo cha Umwagiliaji (*Agricultural Irrigation*)	2010	978-9987-07-033-6
53.	Jifunze Kustawisha **Mpunga** (*How to Grow Paddy*)	2010	978-9987-07-026-8
54.	Jifunze Kustawisha **Karanga** (*How to Grow Groundnuts*)	2010	978-9987-07-027-5
55.	Jifunze Kustawisha **Ufuta** (*How to Grow Simsim*)	2010	978-9987-07-040-4
56.	Jifunze Kustawisha **Mikorosho** (*How to Grow Cashewnuts*)	2010	978-9987-07-023-7
57.	Jifunze Kustawisha **Minazi** (*How to Grow Coconuts*)	2010	978-9987-07-041-1
58.	Kilimo cha **Pamba** Tanzania (*The Agriculture of Cotton in Tanzania*)	2010	978-9987-07-022-0
59.	Jifunze Kustawisha **Pareto** (*How to Grow Pyrenthrum*)	2010	978-9987-07-025-1
60.	Jifunze Kustawisha **Mimea ya Matunda** (*How to Grow Fruit Crops*)	2010	978-9987-07-024-4
61.	Mazao ya Viungo (*Spice Crops*)	2010	978-9987-07-029-9
62.	Jifunze Kustawisha **Uyoga** (*How to Grow Mushrooms*)	2010	978-9987-07-031-2
63.	Jifunze Kustawisha **Michikichi** (*How to Grow Palm Oil Plants*)	2010	978-9987-07-028-7
64.	Magonjwa ya Mifugo (*Diseases of Livestock*)	2010	978-9987-07-045-9
65.	Malisho ya Mifugo (*Pastures of Livestock*)	2010	978-9987-07-036-7
66.	Historia ya Kilimo Tanzania (*The History of Agriculture in Tanzania*)	2014	978-9987-07-043-5

67.	Kanuni 13 za Kupata Ngozi Bora *(13 Principles of Making Better Hides and skins)*	2014	978-9987-07-050-3
68.	**Kahawa** Tanzania *(Coffee in Tanzania)*	2015	978-9987-426-18-8
69.	Mwongozo wa Kilimo Bora cha **Kahawa** *(A Guide to Modern Coffee Farming)*	2015	978-9987-426-22-5
70	Changamoto za Maendeleo ya Mkoa wa Kagera *(The Challenges of Development of Kagera Region)*	2015	978-9987-07-006-0
71.	Mwongozo wa Ufugaji Bora wa **Nyuki** *(A Guide to Modern Bee Keeping)*	2016	978-9987-07-060-2
72	Mwongozo wa Ufugaji Bora wa **Samaki** *(A Guide to Modern Fish Farming)*	2016	978-9987-07-51-0